BUILD YOUR OWN
80286
IBM® COMPATIBLE
AND SAVE A BUNDLE

AUBREY PILGRIM

TAB TAB BOOKS Inc.

Blue Ridge Summit, PA

FIRST EDITION
SECOND PRINTING

Library of Congress Cataloging in Publication Data

Pilgrim, Aubrey,
Build your own 80286 IBM compatible and save a
bundle.

Includes index.
1. Microcomputers–Design and construction–Amateurs'
manuals. 2. Intel 80286 (Microprocessor)–Amateurs'
manuals. I. Title.
TK9969.P55   1988   621.391'6   87-33508

ISBN 0-8306-0331-X
ISBN 0-8306-3031-7 (pbk.)

Questions regarding the content of this book
should be addressed to:
Reader Inquiry Branch
TAB BOOKS Inc.
Blue Ridge Summit, PA 17294-0214

Contents

Acknowledgments

Most of the products in the assembling of an AT were furnished by Paramount Electronics, 1155 Tasman Dr., Sunnyvale, CA 94089, (408) 734-2135.

Introduction

If you have been on a desert island, completely cut off from civilization, you probably have not heard about IBM's new PCs. Except now they are not called PCs anymore; they are called PS/2, for Personal Systems/2. Before the machines were introduced, there were rumors that they would be "clone killers," but after seeing them, most vendors don't regard PS/2s as the fearsome beasts first imagined. In fact, they seem rather tame, and the consensus is that clones will survive and probably prosper. If you have been delaying the purchase of a computer because of the rumors, wait no longer. The clones and compatibles are alive and well and you can fully expect to see them remain that way.

Some of you might still be undecided about buying or building an 80286 clone because of the new IBM PS/2 computers. Chapter 1 gives an in-depth description and comparison of the new IBM computers and clones. The standard-size clone AT, the "Baby" AT, and the Single Board Computers (SBC) that use a backplane are discussed. Using these comparisons and descriptions, you will be able to make a more informed choice.

NOT NECESSARY TO BE AN ELECTRONIC ENGINEER

You might be hesitant as to whether you can build your own computer, but no electronic experience or any special expertise or skills will be required. You will only need a pair of pliers, a couple of screwdrivers, and to follow simple instructions.

If you decide to acquire a clone, you can buy a "bare bones" system, and this book will show you how to add to it or configure it to your needs. You can also buy the individual components and assemble them yourself. This book has some closeup photographs, showing what is inside an 80286 and step-by-step instructions on how to assemble one.

Even if you already have an IBM PC, XT, or an XT clone, you should think seriously about upgrading it to an 80286-based machine. It is very easy to do; just pull out your old mother board and install a Baby AT mother board. This will allow your computer to process data two to four times faster. It will also allow you to use the newer boards that have been developed for the AT.

The new OS/2 operating system is supposed to be released in early 1988. Many programmers have beta versions and are already busy writing new programs for it. The OS/2 will allow an 80286-based machine to access up to 16 megabytes of extended memory. It will also allow an 80286-based machine to address one gigabyte of virtual memory and run several programs at the same time in protected mode. At present, DOS 3.2 cannot handle a hard disk larger than 32 megabytes. The OS/2 will overcome this barrier and allow 80286-based machines to access gigabytes of hard disk storage.

The new OS/2 and the programs that will be written for it will not benefit PC and XT users. They will be stuck with DOS 3.2 or DOS 3.3. It is easy and inexpensive to upgrade, since all you need is the new mother board. You will be able to re-use present disk drives and most other components. If you build your own, you will get a sense of great satisfaction.

EASY TO BE A COMPUTER OPERATOR

You don't have to be an automotive engineer to drive a car; nor is it necessary to know the detailed operation and physics of an internal-combustion engine. Likewise, you need not be a computer scientist or programmer to use a computer. Take advantage of the many thousands of things that they can do for you.

Thousands of off-the-shelf application programs are very user friendly. A vast amount of RAM memory, up to 16 megabytes, is available using the 80286. What a great leap forward from the 64 K limitation that we had to live with in the CP/M world just a few short years ago!

The Macintosh, with its icons and mouse, has been the easiest and simplest machine to use. New software and technologies will now allow the PC and MS-DOS world to enjoy the same ease of use.

This book shows the step-by-step assembly of an 80286. You will not have to do any soldering or complicated assembly. Again, no special expertise is required. Even if you decide not to assemble your own, by using this book you will know what options are available and what to buy. There are billions of dollars worth of hardware and software that are available. We will give some advice and make some recommendations as to what you will need for your applications.

This book will also briefly explain what goes on inside a computer. Even in this day and age, many people still fear computers. They don't understand how simple they really are. Much of the software is now very user-friendly and easy to use, making the computer easy to use. There is ready-made software for almost any application—this makes the computer a very powerful tool that can save you time, labor, and money.

I mention several companies throughout this book. This does not mean that I am endorsing those companies to exclude their competitors. I have had neither the time nor the opportunity to personally evaluate some major hardware items, such as the many dot-matrix and laser printers. I have sometimes relied on the excellent reviews and tests done by *PC Magazine, PC Tech Journal*, and from articles and reviews in the magazines mentioned in Chapter 14. To keep up with this ever changing technology, I subscribe to over 30 computer magazines. Turn to Chapter 14 now, and subscribe to the free magazines.

I attend most of the computer shows in this country, and I seldom miss a computer swap here in the Bay Area.

I have a close relationship with the people at Paramount Electronics in Sunnyvale. Their facilities and products are represented in most of the photos in this book. I spend a lot of time in their shop. I am grateful to Bill Boutin, Jim Behlen, Anoop Singh and the other people at Paramount for their technical advice and their help with the problems I ran into while researching this book.

If you have been doing without a good computer because of the cost, go out and build your own. You can save money and at the same time learn a lot about this wonderful tool that is changing many lives.

1

The IBM PS/2 Versus the Clones

On April 2, 1987, IBM introduced four new model computers—their Personal Systems/2 (PS/2) line. Before the new products were introduced, many people were quite concerned. There were all kinds of rumors that the new machines would be "clone killers" and would eliminate all of the compatible makers except the largest, such as Compaq. However, after taking a look at the new machines, most of the clone vendors and compatible manufacturers don't seem to be too concerned. Even Apple, with their new Macintosh, compatible, seems to be happy.

Comparatively speaking, the IBM systems are still very expensive. It will be some time before software and operating systems are available for the new IBM line-up. Even when the new software is available, the clones will no doubt be able to find a way to do almost everything that IBM does. And they will do it for about one half to one third less than the cost of the IBM system.

SUMMARY OF NEW IBM MACHINES

Some people might still be concerned about the impact of the new machines on the compatibles. Here is a short table that summarizes the main distinguishing features of the new PS/2 systems and compares the systems to a compatible 80286 system.

Table 1-1. Summary Chart.

	MODEL 30	MODEL 50	MODEL 60	MODEL 80	CLONE AT
CPU	8086	80286	80286	80386	80286
SLOTS	3	3	7	7	8
MAXIMUM RAM	640 K	7 M	15 M	16 M	16 M
FLOPPY DRIVES	3.5" 720 K	3.5" 1.44 M	3.5" 1.44 M	3.5" 1.44 M	3.5", 5.25" 720 K, 1.2 M
LARGEST HARD DRIVE	20 M	20 M	185 M	230 M	1500 M
COST (NO MONITOR)	$1695- $2295	$3595	$5295- $6295	$6995- $10,995	$1000- $6000
MONITOR COST	$250- $2840	$250- $2840	$250- $2840	$250- $2840	$100- $2800

All of the new models make extensive use of surface mount technology, Very Large Scale Integration (VLSI) and Application Specific Integrated Circuit (ASIC) chips. This has allowed IBM to integrate onto the mother board many functions that previously required plug-in boards. They now have built-in ports, floppy drive controllers, display drivers, on-board clocks, and many other functions. This integration and the high-density chips have increased the reliability of the machines and allow them to run cooler, with smaller power supplies and a much smaller overall size. But the built-in functions reduce some of the flexibility that was found in the older machines. If you don't like the display adapter in an older machine, you can change it, perhaps for an EGA or Hercules card. And if a board fails, you can easily replace it. If any of the built-in functions of the new PS/2 models fail, the whole mother board will have to be replaced at a considerably higher cost.

NEW FLOPPY DISK STANDARD

The new standard for floppy disks will be 3½ inch. The 3½-inch floppy used on the Model 30 will format to 720 K. The disks used on the Models 50, 60 and 80 will format to 1.44 M. The 1.44-M drives will be able to read the 720-K disks.

This new standard will cause some problems because most of the software comes from the vendors on 5¼-inch disk. For this reason, IBM is offering an external 5¼-inch drive for $375 that can be used to transfer data from the 5¼-inch disk to the 3½-inch disks. You will also need their software ($33) on a 5¼-inch disk that will allow you to move data from a PC, XT or AT to the new models. A serial port cable is used to tie the two machines together. Then the software will allow the data from the external 5¼-inch drive or a 5¼-inch drive in an older machine to be transferred to a 3½-inch disk. The software works in only one direction. It cannot be used to transfer data from a 3½-inch disk to a 5¼-inch disk.

There are still many programs that are copy protected. Some sort of arrangement can be made to have these companies exchange the 5¼-inch disk software for 3½-inch disk. However, this exchange will probably not be done for free.

OPTICAL DISK DRIVE

An optional optical disk drive can be attached to any of the four models. It can only be attached externally to the Models 30 and 50, but it can be mounted internally or externally on the Models 60 and 80. It is a Write Once Read Many (WORM) type of laser drive. The removable disks can store up to 1.6 gigabytes on the Models 60 and 80. The drive sells for $2950.

I discuss optical drives in more detail in Chapter 6.

THE MICRO CHANNEL

The Models 50, 60 and 80 use a new bus system called the Micro Channel. This is completely incompatible with the standard PC bus. The expansion slot connector contacts and mating adapter contacts have 50 mil (.05 inches) spacing. This allows the slot connectors to be about 60 percent smaller than those on the standard PC bus. IBM says that this new design allows more efficient data entry and exit. Look at the edge connector in Fig. 1-1 compared to the Micro Channel.

There are billions of dollars worth of plug-in boards and other hardware that was developed for the standard PC bus. Many vendors, manufacturers and users have large stockpiles of these boards and hardware. None of it can be used on the Micro Channel of the Models 50, 60 or 80 unless someone develops some kind of adapter and cable system that will allow them to be used externally. But that may be more trouble and expense than it is worth.

IBM has set itself apart from the rest of the personal computer market. Obviously, they hope that they can force everyone to buy only IBM products. Many people in the industry have stated that the new changes are unnecessary and that they don't provide many more benefits than what is already available at a much lower price.

IBM created a new standard in 1981 with the introduction of the PC. For a short time they dominated the market, but the clones soon began gnawing away at the lion's share that IBM enjoyed. The clones did this by being innovative and offering more for less. They came up with better keyboards, more memory on board, 8 MHz turbo speed instead of the standard 4.77 MHz, and many more improvements. Being small, the clones could implement changes almost overnight. In many cases it took the

Fig. 1-1. Board in upper photo has standard-edge card connector; board in the lower photo has the small Micro Channel edge connector.

lumbering IBM more than a year to bring their products up to the same level of the clones. The point is that competition from the clones forced changes and improvements. Without this competition, the personal computer technology might today be little more than what we had in 1981.

I hope that IBM has not closed all the loopholes with their 100-or-so patents on the new machines so that the clones can continue to compete and force changes and innovations.

MODEL 30

The IBM PS/2 equivalent to the PC-XT is the Model 30, with an 8086 CPU instead of the 8088. Since the 8086 is a true 16-bit CPU, it runs most programs about twice as fast as the 8088. It will also run at 8 MHz instead of the 4.77-MHz speed of the IBM PCs.

The 8086 CPU was available in 1981 when IBM introduced the first PCs. There was some criticism of IBM for not choosing the superior 8086 instead of the 8088. But at that time, almost all of the available software was written for 8-bit CP/M machines. The 8088 takes two 8-bit chunks of data at a time and processes it, so it was a reasonable choice at that time.

The Model 30 is the only one of the new machines that is still partially hardware-compatible with the present PCs. It retains the standard PC bus and slot connectors so that most of the existing PC and XT plug-in boards can be used on this machine. None of the plug-in boards developed for the AT with the extra 16-bit data bus can be used on any of the new IBM PS/2 machines.

The Model 30 has only three slots, but most of the standard functions are built into the mother board. It has a built-in serial port, a parallel port, a pointing-device port for a mouse or other device, a Multicolor Graphics Array (MCGA) for driving a monitor, a floppy disk controller, and 640 K of RAM.

The footprint of the Model 30 is considerably smaller than that of the PCs. It is only 4 inches high, 16 inches wide and 15.6 inches deep. Since it is only four inches high, the plug-in boards are mounted horizontally instead of vertically as in the older systems. Figure 1-2 shows a side view

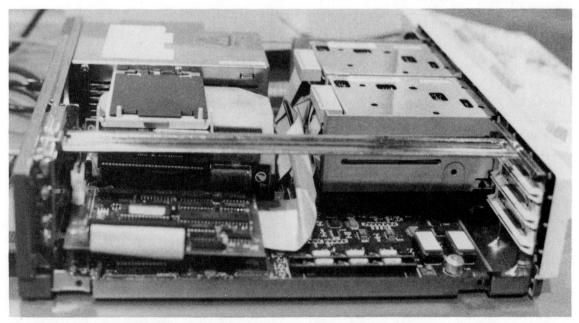

Fig. 1-2. Side view of a PS/2 Model 30.

of the Model 30 with a half-card controller for the hard disk. The plug-in hard disk card can be plugged into these slots to increase hard disk storage above the 20 megabyte maximum that IBM specifies.

A Model 30 with two 3½-inch 720-K floppy drives will cost $1695. One with a 20-M hard disk and a single floppy drive costs $2295. These prices do not include a monitor.

MODEL 50

IBM is offering two models to replace the AT, Models 50 and 60. These use the 80286 CPU, running at 10 MHz. The Model 50 is a desktop unit that is only 5.5 inches high, 14.2 inches wide and 16.5 inches deep.

The Model 50 has one megabyte of RAM on board, built-in ports, and a built-in Video Graphic Array (VGA). This VGA is a VLSI chip that has 12,750 transistors in it.

The Model 50 has three 16-bit expansion slots and a 94-watt power supply. With a single 1.44-M floppy drive and a 20-M hard disk, the Model 50 costs $3595.

The 80286 CPU is capable of addressing 16 M of RAM, but the overall size of the Model 50 limits it to three expansion slots. Because of this limitation, its memory can only be expanded to 7 M. The small case size also presents the addition of a second hard disk, but IBM offers optional external hard disks, optical disks, and streaming tape drives for most of the models.

MODEL 60

Only the monitor and keyboard of the Model 60 sit on the desktop. The electronics and disk drives are mounted in a floor-standing tower. Like the Model 50, it uses the 80286 at 10 MHz and has the same built-in functions. One major difference is that it has seven 16-bit slots and a 207-watt power supply. It can also accommodate a second hard disk or one that is larger than the one used on the Model 50. With one 1.44-M floppy drive and a 44-M hard disk it costs $5295. With a 70-M hard disk it costs $6295. A second 44-M hard drive can be had for $1395, or a second 70-M for $2395. A 115-M hard disk can be installed for an extra $3495.

MODEL 80

The Model 80 is an 80386 CPU-based computer. Like the Model 60, only the monitor and keyboard sit on top of the desk. The Model 80 is very similar to the Model 60 in outward appearance. They both have the same dimensions: 23.5 inches high, 6.5 inches wide and 19 inches deep. The floor-standing towers of the Models 60 and 80 have extended brackets on the bottom (at the front and back) that protect them from being tipped over.

The Model 80 has the same built-in ports, VGA, and other functions that the Models 50 and 60 have. It has four 16-bit expansion slots and three 32-bit slots and a 225-watt power supply.

The Model 80 can be configured several ways. Running at 16 MHz with a 44-M hard disk, it costs $6995. With a 70-M hard disk it is $8495. Running at 20 MHz with a 115-M hard disk it will set you back $10,995. None of these prices include a monitor.

NEW MONITORS

All of the new PS/2 models use analog monitors which have much better resolution. The built-in MCGA will drive a monochrome monitor. A monochrome monitor from IBM costs $250. To use a color monitor on the Model 30, you must purchase an analog display adapter that has the IBM Video Graphics Array (VGA) on it. This adapter can also be used on PCs, XTs, ATs and compatibles to allow them to use the new analog monitors. This adapter costs $595. Some monitors, such as the NEC Multisync, can be used with the new PS/2 by means of a cable adapter to change the connector from 9 pins to the IBM 15 pins. A standard monitor and adapter can be used on the Model 30 but not on the Models 50, 60 and 80.

The 14-inch color monitor costs $595 and the 12 inch is $685. The 12-inch monitor costs more because its dot pitch is finer and gives greater clarity to the images. These monitors have a resolution of 640-by-480 in the graphics mode and 720-by-400 in the text mode. This is much better than the standard Enhanced Graphics Adapter (EGA) resolution of 640-by-350.

IBM also has a 16-inch analog color monitor that has a resolution of 1024-by-768. It sells for $1550 but requires an adapter board that sells for an additional $1290 for a total of $2840.

NEW KEYBOARDS

For the third time in as many years, a new keyboard standard has been adopted. The IBM 101 keyboard has been around for some time, but up until now it has been optional. This keyboard has 12 function keys along the top and separate cursor keys between the right hand numbers and the main keys.

Once again, they have moved **Esc,** \, and several other keys to different locations. These keys are used quite often. Indeed, I am not a very good typist in the first place and it seems like every time I buy a new keyboard, I have to learn all over again.

Many people have bought keyboard overlays for programs such as Framework II or WordStar. They will not be able to use them with the new keyboard.

DOWNWARD COMPATIBILITY

The new IBM machines will be able to run all of the software on the market today. They will also have certain proprietary functions embedded or built-in to the mother board to allow them to run specialized software that will be developed in the future. It has been reported that IBM has applied for over 100 patents for the technology in their new machines. It will be more difficult for the clones to legally duplicate this technology. Nonetheless, several manufacturers are already advertising plug-in boards that will perform many of the IBM built-in functions.

NEW MANUFACTURING TECHNOLOGY

IBM used the latest manufacturing technology in producing their new machines. Automation enables a new machine to come off the assembly line about once every minute. Surface Mount Technology (SMT) allows components on both sides of the boards. Some SMT components are four times smaller than standard components. This allows many more functions to be integrated on a board.

The Models 30 and 50 have no bolts or screws. The cases are plastic and snap together, and the components plug into sockets and connectors. One of these machines can be taken apart and re-assembled in minutes.

COSTS AND PRICES

IBM was not the first computer manufacturer to use this type of technology. Apple built a modern plant for the production of their original Macintosh. It produced a machine every 27 seconds. The estimated cost to Apple of building a Macintosh is $150. When Macintoshes first went on the market, some Apple officials wanted to sell them for about $1900. However, that price would have undercut some of their other products, so they settled on a price of about $2400.

It has been estimated that it costs IBM about $100 to produce the new PS/2 machines. Of course, a lot of money went into research, building the new factory, and overhead. They do have lots of salespeople, managers, robots, and others to support. However, even counting all the overhead and development costs, I suspect there is a lot more ''gravy'' than ''meat'' in the announced prices of these new machines.

Other than being a bit smaller, these new machines offer very little more than the clones have already. In many cases, the clones provide more memory, more hard disk capability, and much more flexibility than the new machines. The clones provide all this computing power for about one half the cost of the comparable IBM machines.

Since they reflect a fairly large profit margin, the prices of the new machines will probably go down some after the initial newness wears off. Some of the people who are buying the new IBMs are like the people who must have a new model car every year. I drive a beat-up, ten-year-old car. To be honest, I wish I could afford a new $20,000 car every year, but my old heap gets me any place I want to go, and its paid for. Besides, if I had an extra $20,000, I would probably spend it on computer goodies.

The new IBM models are pretty, and the IBM logo is a great status symbol. In addition, IBM provides quality products, but they will never equal the performance-to-price ratio of the clones.

To be perfectly honest, I must confess that I lust in my heart for one of the new Model 80s. But alas, I will have to get by with my 80286 clone with a 60-M hard disk for another few months. Then I am going to build an 80386 machine that will outperform the Model 80. It will only cost me about one third of the $10,995 that the Model 80 costs.

NEW DOS 3.3 AND OS/2

A new DOS, version 3.3, has been released, but it has only a few commands that are not in version 3.2. It supposedly offers quicker performance and allows multiple 32-M hard disk partitions. DOS 3.2 costs $75; 3.3 will cost $120, or $75 for an upgrade if you are a registered owner of 3.2.

The new DOS that everyone has been waiting for will be called OS/2 for Operating System/2. It is scheduled for release in early 1988. It will allow the use of Windows, which IBM has endorsed, multi-tasking, and direct addressing of up to 16 M. It will still run almost all existing DOS software. The cost of OS/2 will be $325.

SOME CAPABILITIES OF THE 80286

The 80286 CPU has over 120,000 transistors. When installed in an AT-type computer, it is more powerful than some of the minicomputers were a few years ago. It can run almost all of the four billion dollars worth of off-the-shelf software that was designed for MS-DOS or PC-DOS. It runs this software two to four times faster than the PC or XT. Not enough software has the capability to take full advantage of the 80286 capabilities to do multi-tasking (run in protected mode) and directly address 16 megabytes of memory, but new software is being introduced every day. The new OS/2 that is scheduled to be introduced in early 1988 will be able to tap most of the vast inherent capabilities of the 80286.

HARDWARE

There is also about four billion dollars worth of compatible hardware such as plug-in boards, monitors, keyboards and other peripherals and options available for the 80286. More new products are being developed every day. There are about 10 million IBM PCs, XTs, ATs, and compatibles in use today. The clone makers are not going to abandon this large market. I fully expect to see the market grow in spite of IBM's new standard.

ASSEMBLING YOUR OWN 80286-BASED COMPUTER

You might expect that a machine that utilizes the power and versatility of the 80286 would be very complex and difficult to assemble. Actually, it is less difficult to put together than some of the early PC-XTs. This book will explain how you can assemble one of these powerful systems for less than half the cost of an equivalent IBM machine. You can even beat the cost by at least one third of one of the prominent brand-name compatibles such as Compaq.

I recently retired after several years with Lockheed Missiles and Space Company as a Quality Assurance Engineer. One of my duties was to recommend and order all of the computers and supplies for my department. A little over a year ago I submitted an order for an IBM PC-AT with an EGA color monitor and driver. The cost for the system was a little over $9000. My boss rejected the order and the department had to make do with the two IBM PC-XTs that I had ordered about three years earlier for $5000 each.

Today I can buy an equivalent AT clone with the EGA for about $1500. I can buy a monochrome AT clone system for about $900. I can buy an XT clone system for about $500.

In all fairness, the IBM PC systems *have* been reduced. The $9000 IBM PC-AT EGA system can now be purchased for about $5000. The IBM PC-XT system that cost $5000 four years ago now costs about $2000. However, the XT is being phased out, and IBM is now concentrating on their four new models. Some dealers who had a large inventory of the old XTs are giving a fairly large discount on them. One local dealer recently advertised an IBM PC-XT for $699. However, there was an asterisk after the price, and further down in the ad the asterisk explained that this price was good only if a complete system was ordered. This system included a color monitor, a 20-M hard disk and several other options that added up to almost $2000.

WHY BUY AN 80286 COMPUTER?

Most kinds of businesses require a computer. Depending on the type of business, you might be able to get by with a PC, an XT, or even an Apple. There are now many Point Of Sale (POS) systems that are ideal for small- to medium-sized businesses. They usually have a cash drawer that is tied into a computer. Some might have bar code readers, scanners, and printers. The system can automatically keep track of your sales, inventory, and much more.

If you have a fairly large business or office with large data collection centers, you need a computer such as the 80286, with a large hard disk. You could also use an 80286 to your advantage if you are doing scientific research or investigations; programming, networking, multi-tasking, multi-using, or graphics; Computer Aided Design, Computer Aided Manufacturing, Computer Aided Engineering, or Computer Aided Integration (CAD/CAM/CAE/CAI); Robotics; machine vision; voice data, and thousands of other computer applications.

HOME USE

A few years ago it would have been very difficult to justify buying a $10,000 AT for home use, but now you can buy one for about $1500. I paid $1600 for my first home computer, a Morrow CP/M with 64 K of memory and two single-sided floppy disk drives. I now have an AT compatible with a 60-M hard disk and one megabyte of memory. My little Morrow was like a Model T when compared to my AT, which is more like a plush Cadillac.

I don't really need all the power and facilities that I have on my computer. A person who owns a Ferrari that will do 150 miles an hour doesn't need all that power either, but it sure makes him feel good to know that it is there. I have never driven a Ferrari, but I suppose that in some small measure I get a similar feeling from the performance of my computer. And it costs a helluva lot less.

There are many reasons to have a computer at home. I do a lot of letter writing, but my handwriting is so bad that even I have trouble reading it. I have a typewriter, but I am not a very good typist. With a computer I can easily correct errors, check for spelling mistakes, re-arrange sentences and paragraphs, automatically center text and do other page formats, print in boldface, and perform many other functions that make writing a pleasure.

You can also use a computer at home to keep track of all of your stocks, bonds, and other assets. There are computer programs that help you make investment decisions. There are also programs to help you do your own taxes and financial planning. Some banks will let you do all your banking from home with a computer and a modem.

SCHOOLS

Schools can save millions of dollars if they would buy the components and assemble their own systems. Students could even assemble the computers as part of the learning process. They would learn firsthand what was inside the machine and learn the basics of upgrading or reconfiguring the system.

I worked with engineers for several years. They could operate computers very well, but many of them had no idea at all as to what was inside the box. If they needed to upgrade or had to have the system reconfigured, they usually had to call in a high-priced consultant. After you have finished this book, you will know what is inside the box. You won't need a consultant. In fact, you could even become a consultant. Moreover, you will probably know more than many who call themselves consultants.

A NEW ERA

The world has gone through several significant ages in the past, such as the Stone Age, the Bronze Age, and the Iron Age. We are in the dawn of a new age, the Computer Age. Some people are still trying to ignore computers and refuse to get involved. Computers are not going to go away. They are going to be leading the parade of high technology for years to come. Those who refuse to join the parade are going to be left behind.

On the whole, I don't believe that the new IBM PS/2 system will have any great impact on the clones. The present systems will be around for some time. They can do everything that the PS/2s can do and at a more reasonable cost. If you didn't care about cost, you have probably already bought an IBM. In the next chapter we will show you how to assemble your own powerful 80286 computer and save a bundle of money.

2

How to Assemble an 80286

Although IBM will no longer manufacture the PCs and XTs, it is expected that they will continue to market the IBM PC-XT 286 (Baby AT) and their standard PC-AT. Depending on configuration, the 286 XT costs from $3900 to more than $6000. The PC-AT can cost from $4000 up to $8000. You can assemble an equivalent compatible clone for less than half of what any of these IBMs cost.

Assembly does not require any special expertise or electronic knowledge. It requires no soldering; you need only a pair of pliers, a screwdriver, and about an hour to do the job. And you can save $1000 to $5000.

PARTS NEEDED TO ASSEMBLE YOUR 80286

Many of the basic parts used in the XTs and the ATs are the same. The mother board and case of the standard AT is larger than the XT, but the mother board for the Baby AT is the same size as the XT mother board, and is directly interchangeable.

Here is a list of the basic parts and approximate cost:

Item	Cost
Case	$ 75-125
Power supply	90-135

Item	Cost
Mother board	$ 350-750
Hard & floppy	
Disk controller	180-250
Monitor board	80-400
Monitor	99-600
Multifunction board	75-200
Floppy drive (360 K)	50-125
Floppy drive (1.2 M)	125-150
Floppy drive (3.5")	125-150
Hard disk drives	
(20 M to 150 M)	325-1550
Keyboard	60-90
Total	**$1634-4525**

As you can see, there can be quite a large variation in the cost, depending on the particular configuration you want. There is also a large variation in cost between various dealers. Some of the high-volume dealers charge much less than the smaller ones, so it will pay for you to shop around and compare prices. These figures are rough approximations—the market is so volatile that the prices can change overnight. You should even call or check out the prices advertised in magazines before ordering, because often, the ads have to be made up one or two months before the magazine is published, and the prices could have changed considerably.

I listed several options in the list that are not absolutely necessary for operating a "bare bones" system. It is possible to buy a minimum system for less than $1000. If you are short of cash or if you don't need a lot of goodies at this time, you can buy such a system and add to it later.

The open architecture of the PC allows thousands of different configurations. About four billion dollars worth of hardware has been developed for the PCs. The standard AT has eight slots; some of the Baby ATs might have one or two slots less. These slots will accept most of the available boards. All of the slots have 62-pin connectors for the standard PC bus, but there are additional 36-pin connectors in front of six of the slots. These connectors are for the 16-bit data lines that are needed by the 80286.

The big differences in the above prices are for the mother boards, the monitors, and the hard disk drives. Depending on the dealer, I have seen both Baby AT and standard AT mother boards for as little as $350 and as high as $750. A monochrome monitor can be purchased for as little as $99. A high-resolution Enhanced Graphics monitor might cost from $250 up to $600. An Enhanced Graphics Adapter (EGA) board to drive this monitor might cost from $180 up to $400. A 20 M hard disk drive can be purchased for as little as $325. There are high-capacity hard disks that can store from 40 M to 750 M. A 40-M drive might cost as little as $500, while the 750-M drive can cost over $7500.

COMPATIBILITY

One of the most critical factors determining compatibility with IBM's AT is the Basic Input/Output System (BIOS). To be compatible, a clone must use a system that accomplishes the same tasks as the IBM BIOS. This system, stored in Read Only Memory (ROM), must emulate the IBM system, but must not be a copy. It would be quick and easy to exactly copy an IBM BIOS with an EPROM burner, but this would violate IBM's copyrights and patents. If a company did this, you can be sure that IBM's lawyers would rightfully and immediately be knocking on their door. Two companies, Phoenix Technologies of Massachusetts and the Award Software Company of Los Gatos, in the Silicon Valley, have each developed a legal BIOS that is almost perfectly compatible with IBM.

Ordinarily, you shouldn't have to worry too much about the BIOS, or most of the other components on the mother board. Usually the mother board is completely stuffed and ready to go when you buy it. In some cases, you have an option of adding up to one megabyte of RAM memory to the mother board.

WHERE TO GET COMPONENTS

I live in San Jose, the heart of the Silicon Valley. There is a computer show or swap here almost every weekend. I usually take a pad and pencil with me and walk around to the various booths and check out the prices. When I decide on something, I usually do a bit of haggling. It also helps to wait until the show is almost over; many of the dealers will sell the components at almost no profit rather than have to bundle everything up and carry it back to their store. A knowledgeable person can make some very good deals.

If you don't live near a large city, there are several mail order houses that will ship the units to you. Many computer magazines carry their ads. (Some recommended computer magazines are listed in Chapter 14.) There could be some risk in ordering from the smaller mail order houses. The Far East companies that manufacture most of the components work on a slim profit margin. They don't spend too much money and time on testing and quality control. Bill Boutin is a manager at Paramount Electronics in Sunnyvale, California. They import many of these computer components.

He says that a couple of years ago, 30 to 40 percent of the boards that he received had some sort of defect. He had several technicians who tested all of the boards before they were sold, but some defective boards still managed to slip through.

Because of the time and labor involved in the testing, Jim Behlen, the chief engineer of Paramount, developed an automatic tester for PCs and XTs. It can check out every circuit and component on the mother board and several peripherals in a few minutes. He is now working on a similar tester for 80286 and 80386 machines. As far as I know, no other test instrument like this one exists. I describe it in more detail in Chapter 15.

The Far East manufacturers have identified and eliminated some of the defects that were present in the early boards, but a fairly high rate of defective boards are still shipped. Some of the smaller importers work on a shoestring budget, so they cannot afford to do any testing of the boards. Many of them do not even open the packages before they sell them, but most of these small vendors will promptly replace any component that proves to be defective.

PUTTING A SYSTEM TOGETHER

As I mentioned earlier, you will need two screwdrivers, a flat-blade and a Phillips, and a pair of pliers. It would help if you also have a pair of long-nose pliers and some nut drivers.

Figure 2-1 shows all of the components needed for a basic system. Before I install the system, I lay everything out on a bench and connect it together. I then apply power to make sure that everything is working. This makes troubleshooting easier if something is wrong.

Figure 2-2 is a picture of a standard size AT mother board. Figure 2-3 shows the power supply being connected to the mother board. These power supply connectors are usually marked P8 and P9. Figure 2-4 is a close-up of these two connectors. *Note that the two black wires on each connector must be adjacent to each other in the center of the connection.* It's very important that these connectors be connected properly, otherwise the components on the mother board could be severely damaged when power is applied.

Figure 2-5 shows a 34-wire controller cable being attached to a hard disk connector. This cable will have a colored wire on one side which indicates pin one. The edge connector on the hard disk will usually have a "1" or a "2" etched on the board. (All of the even numbers of the edge connector are on one side of the board and all of the odd numbers are on the other side.) Plug the cable in so that the colored wire goes to the end of the edge connector marked "1" or "2." In some cases,

Fig. 2-1. Components needed for an AT.

the cable will have a key in it and there will be a slot in the edge connector so that it can only be plugged in properly.

It is not shown too clearly in these pictures, but there is also a 20-wire data cable that plugs into an edge connector on the back of the hard disk. This cable also has a colored wire that indicates pin one. Use the same procedure as above: look for an etched "1" or "2" on the edge connector and plug it in so that the colored wire goes to that side of the connection.

Figure 2-6 shows the power cable from the power supply being attached. There are four identical cables from the power supply, so it is possible to power any combination of two hard disks and two floppy disks. The connectors on these cables are shaped so that they can only be plugged in the proper way.

Figure 2-7 shows the other ends of the controller and data cables for the hard disk. These ends are attached to the controller board. This AT controller board can control two floppy drives and two hard disk drives. The controller card has two 34-pin connectors and two 20-pin connectors. The 34-pin connector toward the back of the board is for the cable to the floppy disk drives. When plugged in properly, the colored wire will be on top. There will be two connectors on this cable for two floppy drives. This cable is shown in Fig. 2-8. Note that the connector on the end is split and twisted. This connector goes to floppy disk drive A. If a second floppy

Fig. 2-2. A standard size AT mother board.

drive is used, the connector in the middle plugs into it. These cables also
have a colored wire that indicates pin one and the edge connector on the
floppy drive will be marked with a "1" or a "2."

Refer back to Fig. 2-7. The 34-wire cable for the hard disks can also
have two connectors. Both connectors on this cable will be wired
identically. If you have two hard disks, either one can be plugged into either hard disk. Connect the cable to the controller board through the 34-pin
connector toward the front of the board. The colored wire should be on
top. There are two 20-pin connectors on the controller board for the data

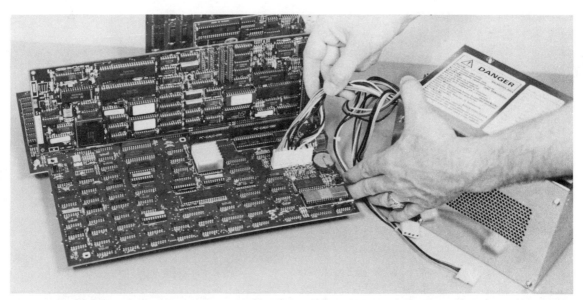

Fig. 2-3. Connecting a power supply to the mother board.

Fig. 2-4. A close-up of the mother board power connectors.

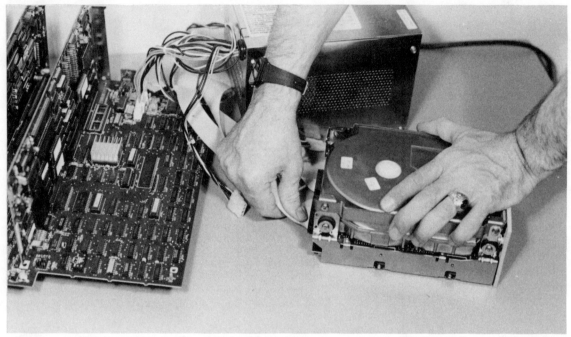

Fig. 2-5. A 34-pin ribbon cable connector being attached to a hard disk.

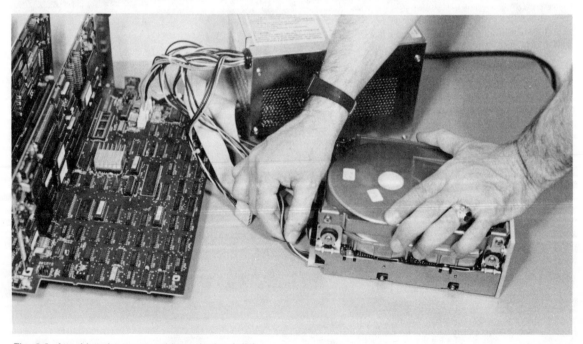

Fig. 2-6. Attaching the power cable to the hard disk.

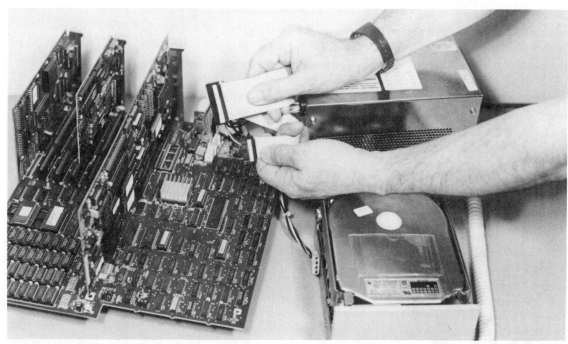

Fig. 2-7. Preparing to attach the hard disk cables to the controller card.

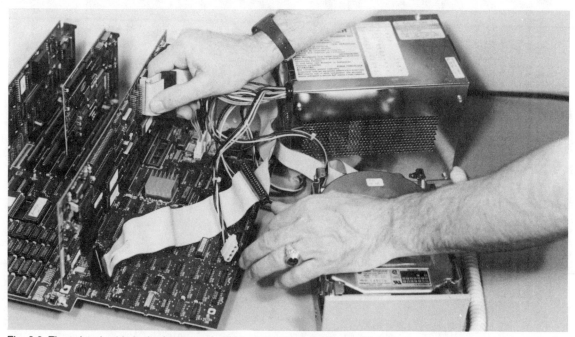

Fig. 2-8. The twisted cable in the foreground will be plugged into the floppy drive A.

cables for the hard disks. The 20-pin connector toward the back and adjacent to the 34-pin hard disk connector is for the first hard disk. If you have a second hard disk, a second 20-pin cable should be plugged into the connector toward the front of the board. Again, the colored wire should be on top.

Figure 2-9 shows the hard disk cables connected to the controller board. Figure 2-10 shows a power cable for the floppy disk drive. Figure 2-11 shows the 34-pin connector for the floppy disk drive. Since I show only one floppy, this will be drive A. Figure 2-12 shows the connector attached to the floppy drive.

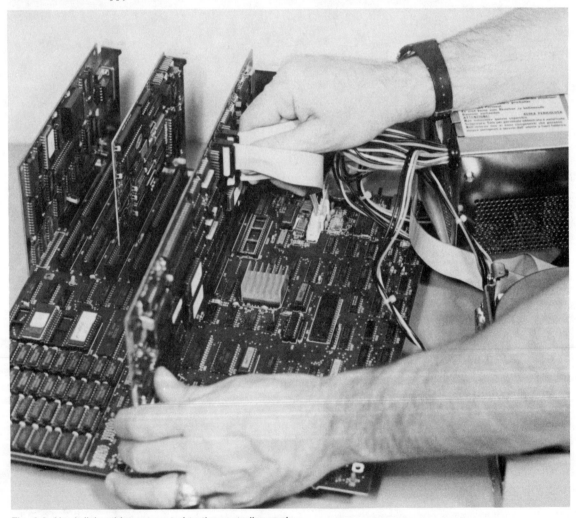

Fig. 2-9. Hard disk cables connected to the controller cards.

Fig. 2-10. A power connector for a disk drive.

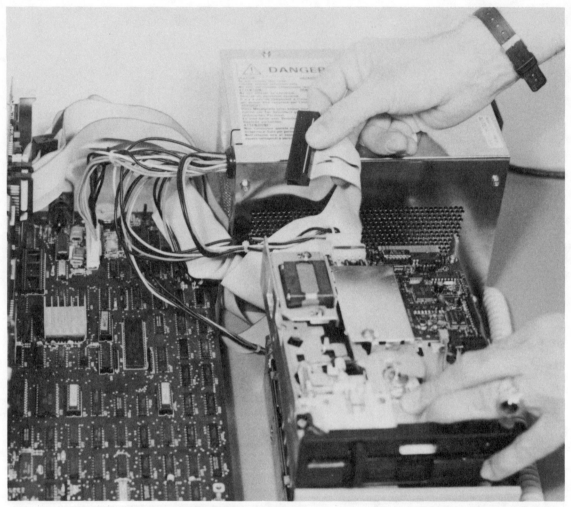

Fig. 2-11. The 34-pin connector for the floppy disk drive A. There are usually two connectors on this cable The one on the end has some twisted wires, which determines drive A.

Figure 2-13 includes a monitor attached to monitor driver card. The card in the center is a parallel port for a printer. You are now ready to apply power to see if everything operates properly. You should test the system for a couple of days before installing it in the case.

Figure 2-14 shows a case with a plastic bag of small parts, the speaker, rails for the disk drives, plastic standoffs for the mother board, and other small pieces of hardware. One of the white plastic standoffs can be seen near the speaker. Near the standoff is a slotted cutout. There are four of these cutouts on the floor of the case. Three black plastic standoffs

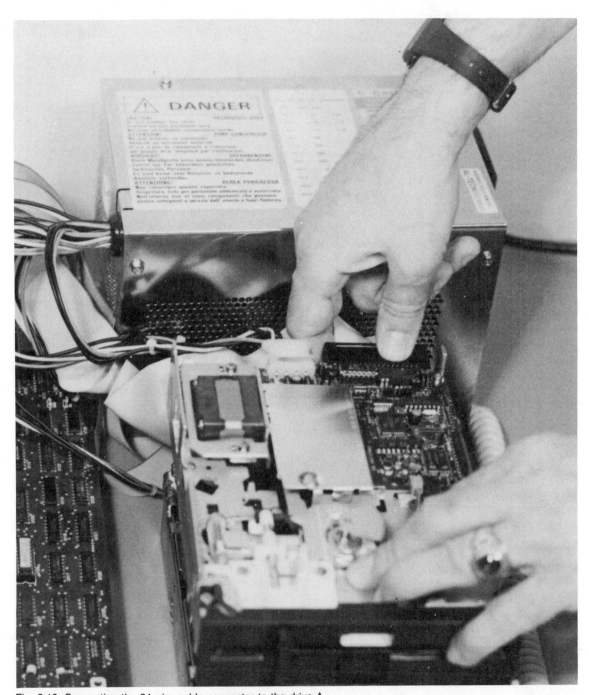

Fig. 2-12. Connecting the 34-wire cable connector to the drive A.

Fig. 2-13. A system connected on the bench for pretesting before final assembly.

are mounted on the floor of the case. They have a slot that accepts the right edge of the mother board.

Figure 2-15 shows the back side of the mother board. Four of the white plastic standoffs have been pressed into holes from the back side. The standoffs have slotted collars. Place the mother board on the floor of the case, position the standoffs over the cutouts, then drop them in and push to the right about a quarter of an inch. The small portions of the cutouts lock the white plastic standoffs in place. Engage the right edge of the mother board in the horizontal slots of the black standoffs. Place a screw in the hole in the center of the front of the mother board and one at the center of the back. These two screws will hold the mother board securely and form a good ground to the case.

Figure 2-16 shows the bottom of the power supply and the bottom of the case. Note that the power supply has two depressed slots and the case has two raised tongues. Place the power supply over the raised tongues and slide it toward the back of the case. Four screws from the back of the case fasten the power supply securely. Figure 2-17 shows the mother board mounted in the case and the power supply connected.

Fig. 2-14. A 286 chassis with the small parts that comes with it.

Figure 2-18 shows a close-up of the power supply connector showing the four black wires in the center as mentioned before. To the left of the power supply connector is the plug-in connector for the keyboard.

Figure 2-19 shows the disk controller card with all the cables attached. Mount the speaker on a bracket with a single screw. Plug the leads from the speaker and the LED power indicator into the pins on the front of the mother board. The leads from the LED for the hard disk indicator should be plugged into the pins on the front of the disk controller card.

Figure 2-20 shows the disk drives and the plastic rails that are attached to them. These rails fit in grooves in the case so that the drives can be slid in and out very easily.

Figure 2-21 shows the small angle brackets that hold the disk drives in place. The angle presses against the rail of the disk drive so that it is secure. The brackets are inaccessible when the cover of the case is installed so that the disks cannot be removed without removing the cover.

Fig. 2-15. The back of the mother board. The white objects are the plastic standoffs.

Fig. 2-16. The bottom of the power supply. Note the slots that receive the raised tongues on the floor of the chassis.

Fig. 2-17. The mother board installed and the power supply cables connected.

The cover has five screws in the back to hold it on, but the keylock has a bracket that holds the case so that it cannot be removed unless it is unlocked.

The keylock performs another useful function. With the power on, the key can be switched to the keyboard lock position and nothing can

Fig. 2-18. A close-up of the power supply connection. Note that the four black wires are in the center.

Fig. 2-19. A disk controller card with all cables connected.

be entered from the keyboard. If you are in the middle of a job, you can lock out the keyboard, take a break, and not worry about someone fooling around with the computer while you are gone.

Figure 2-22 shows a battery pack attached to the end of the power supply. (Double-sided foam tape was used to attach the battery pack.)

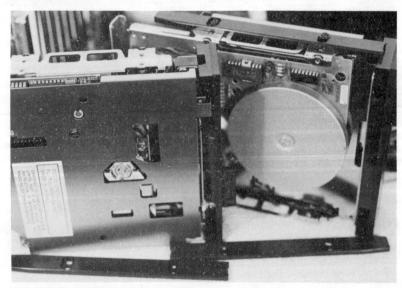

Fig. 2-20. Plastic rails for disk drives.

Fig. 2-21. Small angle brackets, used to hold the disk drives in place.

The BIOS of the AT uses low-current CMOS ROM to hold the system configuration and some of the boot routines. The battery pack used in the IBM PC-AT costs $30 and is only good for about two years. The compatibles and clones use a battery pack with four penlight AA alkaline batteries that cost about $1 each. These batteries last about three years.

Fig. 2-22. A battery pack attached to the case of the power supply with double-sided foam tape.

MOUNTING DISK DRIVES

The original IBM PC had space for two full-height floppy drives. With the release of the XT, you could have one full-height floppy and one full-height 10 M hard disk. The clones soon came out with half-height drives. It then became possible to mount two floppies and two hard disks in this space, but it was rather difficult and time consuming to mount the disk drives on the brackets.

It is considerably easier to mount the disk drives on the standard AT case. There are grooves in the case for plastic rails that attach to the disk drives. The drives are slid in from the front and a small bracket holds them in place.

The standard AT case size is about one inch taller than the PC, so it is possible to mount three half-height drives in the open area. There are three grooves in this area. Two grooves are in the left-hand area so that two half-height hard drives or one full-height hard drive can be mounted there. This area on the left is inaccessible when the cover is installed, but it is not ordinarily necessary to access the hard drives. The cover extends over the small brackets that hold the drives in place. This offers some security in that the drives cannot be removed without the key to unlock the cover.

Figure 2-23 shows a 3½-inch disk sitting in the slot beneath a 5¼-inch floppy. Figure 2-24 shows the extenders and rails that must be used to make it fit in the 5¼-inch slot.

The 3½-inch disk floppy drive will undoubtedly become the new standard. At the present time, the AT can format the disks to 720 K, but I am certain that ATs will soon be configured to use the new 1.44-M format.

Many 3½-inch hard disks are also being used today. They are light and fast. With some of the new technologies that I cover in later chapters, these small hard disks can hold as much as 100 M of data.

BUTTONING UP THE SYSTEM

There are several different types of mother boards. You should be sure to get as much information as possible on any component that you buy. You should be given a small booklet showing the location of the various connectors, switches, and jumpers needed for configuring your system. For instance, you may have two or more serial and parallel ports built into your mother board. In such case, there are usually pins mounted on the mother board that can accept connectors and cables for the ports. Other pins have small shorting bars to enable or disable these ports. Some systems have a switch or pins with a shorting bar for changing the speed from 6 to 8 or 10 MHz. There might also be pins for configuring the board for the type of monitor you will be using. Without the instruction booklet

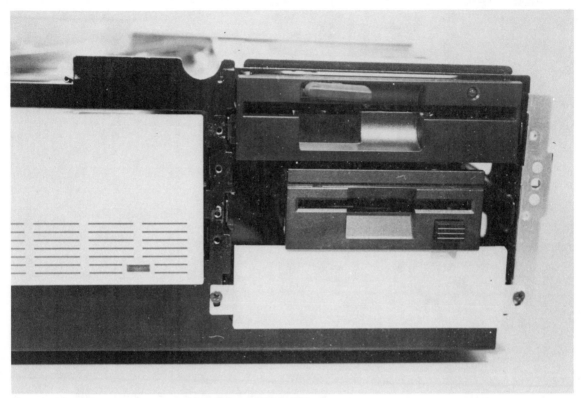

Fig. 2-23. A 3½-inch floppy drive sitting under a 5¼-inch drive.

and diagrams, it might be very difficult to configure your system. Some of the newer mother boards allow many of these configurations to be done externally from the keyboard.

Once the mother board has been configured to your requirements, you can install the plug-in boards and the cover. Before installing the cover, it is a good idea to double check all the cable connections and switch settings. Then plug in the monitor and keyboard. Note that the XT and AT keyboards might look identical, but they are different internally. Many of the keyboards have a small switch on the back that can be set for either the XT or the AT.

A WORD OF CAUTION

I strongly suggest that you buy a power strip that has five or six outlets for all of the peripherals that will be connected to your computer. This is especially important if you are going to use your computer at home. Most homes now have three-wire outlets for polarized plugs that can only be inserted one way. Almost all modern-day printers, monitors, computers,

Fig. 2-24. The extenders and rails needed to make a 3½-inch drive fit in a 5¼-slot.

and other peripherals will have a three-wire plug. If you are using the computer at home and have only two-wire outlets, you might be tempted to cut off the U-shaped grounding part of the connector so that you could plug the connector into a two-wire outlet—*do not do this*. It is possible that some of your units are not isolated from ground, so you might get 110 volts on the case of your printer or some other peripheral. Even if they are isolated, plugging in one or more of your components to the wrong side of the line can cause grounding problems.

The plug-in slots in a two-wire outlet are also polarized. If you look at them closely, you will see that one slot is wider than the other. This slot should be grounded. It will usually have a white wire attached to it. If you followed it back to your fuse box, you might find that it would be grounded to a water pipe or some other common ground that eventually goes to earth ground. The wire that is attached to the narrow slot will be black. This wire should carry 110 volts.

Some older houses (or even some new ones) could have some of their connectors miswired. I live in a fairly new apartment, and I found several outlets in my house that had been miswired. It is an easy matter to check the outlet; most hardware stores have small, inexpensive voltage indicators. These are usually just a small neon bulb which, when plugged into a socket, will light up if there is voltage present. A more versatile alternative is an inexpensive volt-ohmmeter. It is a very handy tool to have around the house for any kind of electrical problem.

If you have a two-wire system in your house, check the outlet to make sure that it is wired properly. You can remove the cover and make sure that the white wire goes to the wider slot. Then buy a power strip and an adapter so that it can be plugged into the two-wire outlet. I suggest that you buy a strip that has surge protection. If you have a refrigerator or other heavy appliances on the line, it can cause a large back surge of voltage when it turns on. These surges can cause glitches that show up as errors in your data.

If you live in an area that has lightning storms, I strongly suggest that you buy protectors for your system. Check with your local hardware or electrical stores. And, it is a good idea to disconnect the power strip during heavy electrical storms.

If you must use your computer and there is a chance of a power outage, you should save your data to disk frequently. Otherwise, if the power goes off even for a split second, all of your data that has not been saved to disk will be lost from RAM memory. It is a good idea to save your data every 10 or 15 minutes because a glitch could cause you to lose all of the data that has not been saved. I discuss power supplies and surge protectors in more depth in Chapter 4.

After you have installed your power strip, you will be ready to turn on the system and start computing.

BARE BONES SYSTEMS

If you don't feel comfortable about assembling your own computer, you can buy a "bare bones" minimum system that has a mother board, monitor board, disk drive boards and disk drives installed. You can then add other components from other sources one at a time. If something goes wrong, it will be fairly easy to determine what it is by unplugging the last board added before the problem appeared. (I will have more to say about problems and their diagnoses in Chapter 15.)

Competition has driven prices so far down that you might not save that much by buying the separate components and starting from scratch. Most vendors will sell a minimum system that has been assembled and tested for just a few dollars more than what the various components would cost if bought separately. This could save you some time and trouble, but you would be missing out on a great learning experience.

BURN-IN AND INFANT MORTALITY

Once you get a system, you should plug it in and let it run for about a week. This burn-in will get rid of most of the infant mortality. If a semiconductor circuit is designed properly, it should last several lifetimes, but if it is defective it will usually go out within the first week of use. Many vendors do a burn-in before they sell a system, but you should still do one yourself. Once the system has successfully passed this first week of use, you shouldn't have much trouble.

3

The Baby AT

Shortly after IBM released their 80286 PC-AT, the Chips and Technology Company of Milpitas began designing VLSI chips that would integrate several of the IBM mother board functions. They were able to design a single chip that could replace as many as 30 chips on the IBM mother board. Using these chips, the size of the mother board could be drastically reduced. The clone makers immediately came out with a Baby AT board that was the same size as the IBM PC-XT. A person could remove the mother board from a standard IBM PC, XT, or one of the compatibles, install the Baby AT mother board, which would immediately upgrade it to the much more powerful AT. Alternately, a person could buy the mother board and standard components and build an AT in a standard PC size case. However, because of the development costs, the board was a bit more expensive than the standard-size AT boards. Many of the Far East companies flooded the market with standard-size mother boards and prices for the larger boards fell dramatically, so not too many of the Baby AT boards were sold.

About a year after the clones came out with the Baby AT, IBM released their own Baby AT mother board and system to replace the aging PC-XT. They called it the PC-XT 286. One difference between the XT and the AT is that the AT is wider, deeper, and about one inch taller than the XT. The extra height of the case allowed manufacturers to design plug-in boards with more components and functions on them. The AT can address up to 16 M of RAM. Plug-in memory boards were designed with as much as 2 M on them, but these boards were necessarily larger at first. With newer technologies, manufacturers are now making smaller boards that will fit in the XT-size cases. The standard PC or XT case size is 19.6 inches wide, 16 inches deep and 5.5 inches high. The standard AT case size is 21 inches wide, 16 inches deep and 6.25 inches high. Several manufacturers are now making special cases that have the same footprint as the XT, but are an inch higher to accommodate the larger boards. These cases have a keylock, and except for their smaller size, are almost identical to the standard AT case.

CONVERTING A PC OR XT INTO AN AT

Figures 3-1 and 3-2 show two Baby 286 boards. They are slightly different. The board in Fig. 3-2 has a notch in front, because some of the

Fig. 3-1. A mother board for a Baby AT. Note that this board has only 7 slots.

XTs have a disk-mounting bracket mounted to the floor of the case. Most XTs have an elevated disk-holding bracket so that the full-size mother board shown in Fig. 3-1 can be used. Another difference is that the board in Fig. 3-1 has seven slots with only three 36-pin, 16-bit data connectors. The mother board in Fig. 3-2 has the standard eight slots with six 36-pin, 16-bit data connectors.

Figure 3-3 shows the underside of the mother board shown in Fig. 3-1. Seven white plastic standoffs, similar to the ones used in the standard AT, have been installed. Two screws, one in front and one in back, secure the mother board and make a good ground to the case. Some of the newer XT cases have been designed to accept these standoffs. For the older style cases, nine plastic or brass standoffs must be used.

Using one of these new boards, an XT can be converted into an 80286 machine in less than 20 minutes. The most difficulty in the entire operation

Fig. 3-2. Another mother board for the Baby AT. Note that it has 8 slots and also that it has a cut out in the front for XT cases that have a bracket for the disk drives.

Fig. 3-3. The underside of the mother board shown in Fig. 3-1. Note the white plastic standoffs.

is removing and replacing the five screws in the back that hold the XT cover on.

Figure 3-4 shows an IBM XT with the cover off, the plug-in boards removed, and the power supply being disconnected. Two screws are then removed and the XT mother board is pulled out. Figure 3-5 shows the case with the XT mother board removed. Note that it was unnecessary to remove the power supply, disk drives or any other components. Figure 3-6 shows the new Baby AT mother board in place. Figure 3-7 shows the disk drive cables being reconnected to the disk controller boards.

Figure 3-8 includes the cables going to the two separate controller boards. The same disk-controller boards that were used in the XT can be used in the AT. One of the controller boards is for the hard disk, and the other is for the floppy drives. These of course use two slots. The standard AT disk controller can control both floppies and the hard disk from a single board, but they cost as much as $200. If your computer setup is not crowded, a floppy controller such as the one shown in Fig. 3-9 can

Fig. 3-4. An IBM XT with the cover and boards removed. The power supply is being disconnected from the mother board.

be bought for as little as $35. A hard disk controller such as the one used in this machine costs as little as $90.

Figure 3-10 shows the new Baby AT with the cover re-installed. In its previous form, as an IBM PC-XT, the computer operated at 4.77 MHz and was limited to 640 K of RAM. Because it was a genuine IBM, it was worth about $2000. (An equivalent compatible would be worth about $1000). With 20 minutes time and a $500 mother board, the machine is now worth about $4000.

If you are converting one of the early model IBM PCs, you should check your power supply. The early PCs came with a 67-watt power supply. You can probably get by with 135-watt supply which costs $50 to $70, but the 150-watt supply is the same size and costs only five to ten dollars more. I recommend that you install the 150-watt supply, especially if you

Fig. 3-5. The case with mother board removed. This is a late model XT with the raised brackets for the standoffs. The earlier cases did not have this feature.

plan to run more than two disk drives and a full complement of plug-in boards.

The AMQ Corporation in Sunnyvale furnished the boards and IBM PC-XT for the pictures. AMQ uses the Baby AT mother board extensively in the excellent portable they manufacture.

BUILDING FROM SCRATCH

You might want to build a Baby AT from scratch. They have about the same performance of the larger standard size AT. In fact, they are better than their larger brother in several respects. They have a smaller footprint, so that take up less desk space. Because of the on-board VLSI, there is less chance of individual chip failures. VLSI also requires less power, so a 150-watt power supply will be sufficient in most cases. The larger AT requires a power supply of about 200 watts.

The disk drives, plug-in boards, monitors, and other peripherals would be the same as for the standard size AT or the XT. Look in any computer

Fig. 3-6. The new Baby AT mother board installed.

Fig. 3-7. Disk drive cables being reconnected.

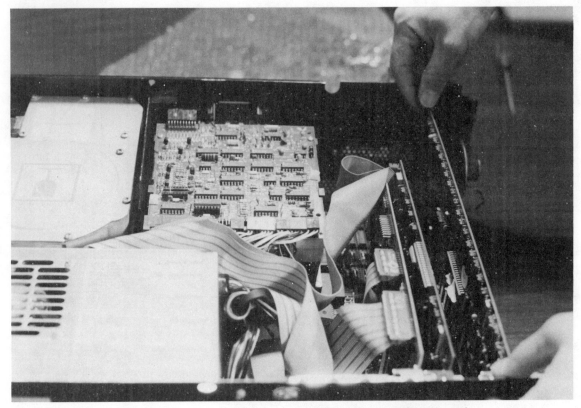

Fig. 3-8. Installing monitor adapter. Note that the same drive-controller plug-in cards were used.

magazine and you will see that there is an abundance of components available at very reasonable prices.

There is a wide variation in the cost of the Baby AT mother boards. I have seen some advertised for as little as $350 and some for as much as $900. Figure 3-11 shows a Far East Baby AT, with no memory, priced at $300. I am not convinced that the higher cost boards are that much better. If you decide to upgrade a PC or XT or build one of these systems, it would pay you to shop around and compare prices.

SINGLE BOARD COMPUTERS

The Faraday Corporation of Sunnyvale and several other companies have designed an AT on a single plug-in board. Figure 3-12 shows a Faraday BUS-AT single board computer. Faraday has used VLSI and Application Specific ICs (ASIC) to put the whole basic AT mother board on a standard-sized, 4.8 by 13.2 inch plug-in board. Figure 3-13 shows it plugged into a backplane, which is just slot connectors with the standard PC bus

Fig. 3-9. A small floppy-disk controller that can be used in XT or AT.

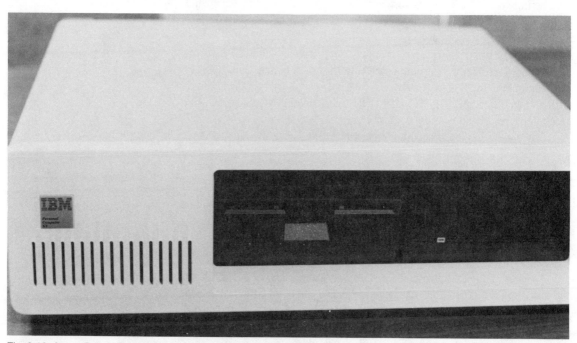

Fig. 3-10. A new Baby AT, now worth about twice what it was before installing the new mother board. The products shown in these photos were furnished by AMQ Corp. of Sunnyvale.

Fig. 3-11. A Far East Baby AT mother board with no memory for $300 in OEM quantities.

connecting them. Notice that some of the connectors on the backplane have the extra 36-pin, 16-bit data connector in front of the standard 62-pin, 8-bit connector.

Figure 3-13 also shows a power supply, disk drives, a controller board, and a multifunction board all connected together on a bench. This system can be mounted in the newer Baby AT cases or on special backplane cases with a small footprint. The Faraday BUS-AT is used in special industrial control instruments.

The address of Faraday Electronics is:

Faraday Electronics
749 N. Mary Ave.
Sunnyvale, CA 94086
(408) 749-1900

ACCELERATOR BOARDS

The new IBM PC introduced in 1981 operated at 4.77 MHz, about the same speed as the CP/M machines. Because the 8088 CPU processed two 8-bit chunks of data at a time, it handled data at almost twice the speed of the CP/M machines. Even at this speed, they were painfully slow when it came to handling large spreadsheet files and some graphics programs. Several manufacturers developed speed-up or accelerator plug-in boards.

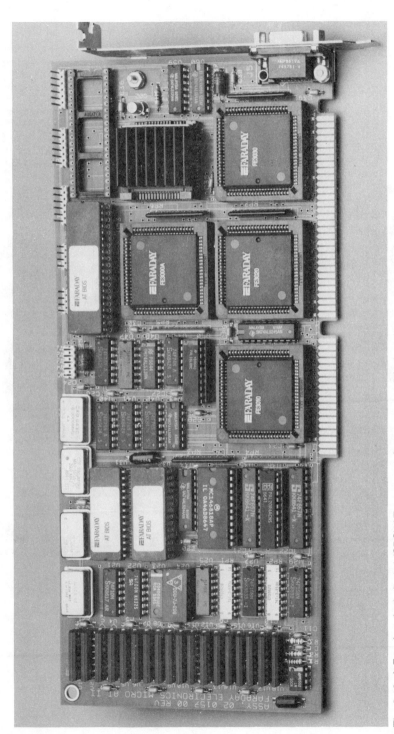

Fig. 3-12. A Faraday single board (SBC) AT computer. It measures 4.8 inches wide and 13.2 inches long.

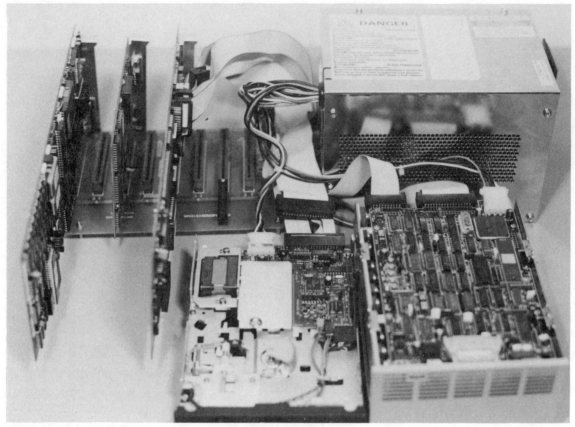

Fig. 3-13. A Faraday single board computer, disk controller, power supply and disk drives connected to a backplane—a complete AT computer.

At about the same time, the clone makers started producing compatible XTs with the Turbo option. With this option, a PC or an XT could operate at as high as 8 MHz.

If you have an older PC or XT and don't want to go all the way up to the 80286, you can add one of these boards. You can increase the speed of your PC or XT for as little as $10 or as much as $1500. However, none of these options will give you all of the power, versatility, and flexibility of a real 80286.

THE NEC V20

The least expensive way to increase the speed of a PC or XT is to remove the 8088 CPU and replace it with an NEC V20. When this chip was first introduced it sold for as much as $40. It now costs as little as $10 at some discount houses.

The NEC V20 CPU is a direct replacement for the 8088. (In fact it is so similar that Intel sued NEC). The V20 handles some types of data a bit faster internally than the 8088. Some early vendors of this chip claimed increases of up to 40 percent, whether you were operating at 4.77 MHz or 8 MHz, but I have not seen this first hand. I bought one and did several benchmark tests. The best I could do was about 10 percent. The type of program used makes quite a bit of difference. Some number-crunching programs give good results; some other programs will show little or no increase in performance.

The NEC company also manufactures a V30 chip that supposedly speeds up the 8086 CPU. The new IBM PS/2 Model 30 uses the 8086.

The V20 and V30 are available from most computer parts and supply stores. Look in any computer magazine for these stores' ads.

PC SPRINT

The PC has several chips on board that perform more than one function. One of these is the 8284 clock chip. The PCs and XTs have a crystal that oscillates at 14.31818 MHz. This frequency is divided by four, to equal 3.58 MHz, and used by the color monitor. The 14.31818 MHz signal is also divided by three, to produce the standard clock rate of 4.77 MHz that controls both the Direct Memory Access (DMA) and the speed and cycling of the CPU and other control chips. The 4.77 MHz is divided by two and sent to a 8253 timer chip that keeps track of the time of day and date and also sends a refresh signal to the DMA.

You could install a higher frequency chip, but this would interfere with all the other functions in the system. The PC Sprint solves the problem by adding an additional 8284 chip and a higher frequency oscillator. The original 8284 is removed and a small board is plugged into the socket. This board has one 8284 in it and a socket for the original 8284 that was removed. The board also has two different crystals, 6.67 MHz and 7.38 MHz, that can be plugged in. Some older PCs may have the 250-nanosecond (ns) RAM, which is much too slow for the higher frequencies. (If you look at your RAM chips, they will usually have a two-digit number that indicates their speed. A 250-ns chip would be marked – 25, a 200-ns chip would be marked – 20. Most of the newer chips are now at least 150 ns. Some of the new 386 machines use 70-ns chips, which are more expensive). You should try the 7.38-MHz crystal first, but, if that causes any problems, try the 6.67 MHz. To operate at frequencies above 5.0 MHz, you must replace your standard 8088 with an 8088-2 or a V20 CPU. The unit also has a switch that can be mounted to the back of the computer to allow you to switch back to the 4.77-MHz mode if needed.

For less than $100 you can almost double the speed of most of your computer operations. Their address is:

PC-Sprint
Exec-PC Inc.
P.O. Box 11268
Shorewood, WI 53211
(414) 242-2173

Here are the addresses of six other fairly low-priced speed-up boards. All of them use the 8088-2 or the V20 and operate in a manner similar to the PC Sprint.

The American Turbo $120
American Computer & Peripheral
270 Croddy Way
Santa Ana, CA 92704
(714) 545-2004

Surprise! $249
Maynard Electronics
400 E. Semoran Blvd. #207
Casselberry, FL 32707
(305) 331-6402

TurboSwitch $149
Megahertz Corp.
2681 Parleys Way
Salt Lake City, UT 84109
(801) 485-8857

Fast88 $149
Microspeed
5307 Randall Place
Fremont, CA 94538
(415) 490-1403

Screamer $199
Microsync
15018 Beltway Dr.
Dallas, TX 75244
(214) 788-5198

87/88 Turbo $149
MicroWay
P.O. Box 79
Kingston, MA 02364
(617) 746-7341

AT-TYPE ACCELERATOR BOARDS

Because they all use the 8088 type CPU, none of the low cost boards above will give you AT type speed. There are several boards that can actually replace your 8088 with a 16-bit CPU. These boards will allow your computer to process data and operate at frequencies from 6 MHz all the way up to 12 MHz.

The Breakthru 286 company makes two such boards: one that operates at 8 MHz for $395, and one that operates at 12 MHz for $595. I ran some benchmark tests on their 8 MHz model (before the 12-MHz model was available). Figure 3-14 shows the Breakthru 286. Figure 3-15 shows the 8088 being removed. The Breakthru 286 comes with a small tool that makes removal very easy.

Figure 3-16 shows the noise suppressor mounted in the 8087 socket. If you have an 8087 coprocessor, it should be removed and mounted in the empty socket on the Breakthru board.

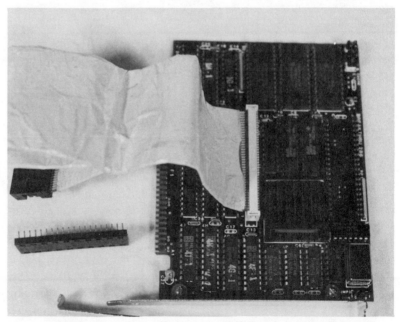

Fig. 3-14. The Breakthru 286 card with an 80286 CPU. It has a cable that plugs into the 8088 socket and a noise suppressor chip that plugs into the 8087 socket.

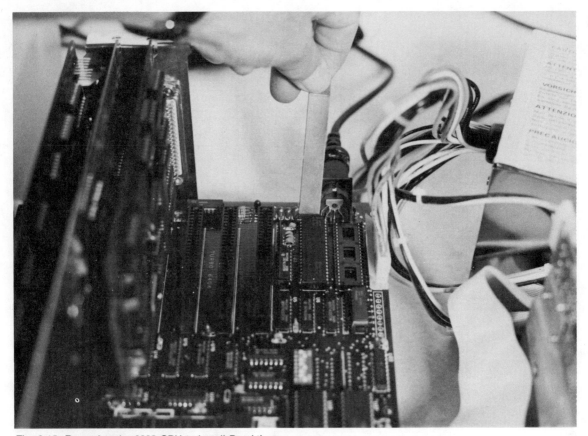

Fig. 3-15. Removing the 8088 CPU to install Breakthru.

Figure 3-17 shows the cable connector plugged into the 8088 CPU socket. This cable will reach any slot on the mother board. I mounted my board in slot number one. Figure 3-18 shows the system set up outside the case on a bench.

Norton's Utilities software has a program called Systems Information, or SI. The SI command causes a check of the BIOS date, the DOS system in use, the number of drives attached, a complete memory allocation report, and the computing performance index relative to the IBM PC. Before I installed the Breakthru, I ran the SI program. It indicated that the PC was rated at 1.0. After installing the Breakthru, I ran the test again. It told me that it now had a computing performance rating of 7.1. The PCSG Company, who makes the Breakthru, claims that it would give a rating of 8.0, but my computer was never able to achieve this performance level.

I made up a little batch file that uses the computer's timing system to check the SI program time with the 8088 and then with the Breakthru.

Fig. 3-16. Noise suppressor installed in 8087 socket.

Here is the batch file program. At the C> or A>, type:

```
copy con clk.bat
time
SI
time
^Z or F6
```

Clk.bat, (for clock), is the name I gave the file. You may name it anything you like. The name should be short, preferably no more than three characters. This little batch file could be modified and used for many time-measuring functions. Just invoke the time command, have the computer run almost any program, then invoke the time command again at the end.

When I typed clk, the computer displayed the current time:

```
Current time is 14:10:48.74.
Enter new time:
```

I then pressed the RETURN or ENTER key twice, as quickly as possible. The displayed time then became the beginning of the test. It ran the test, then displayed:

```
Current time is 14:10:57.20.
```

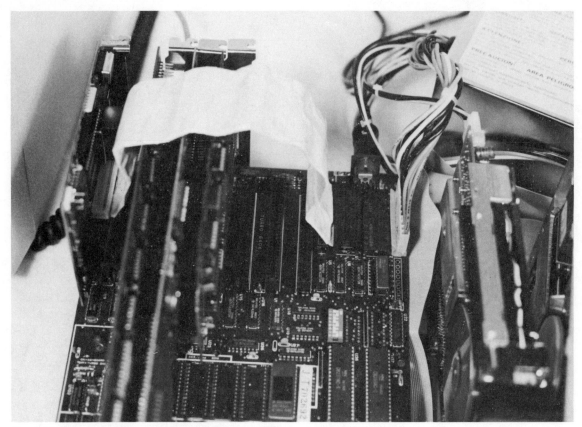

Fig. 3-17. The board with connectors installed.

If you subtract the beginning time from that displayed at the end of the program you find that it took 8.46 seconds to do the test. This was the results with the 8088 CPU.

I then installed the Breakthru and typed clk and test. It came up with:

Current time is 14:18:54.50
Enter new time:

I hit RETURN twice and the program ran and displayed:

Current time is 14:18.57.19

as the ending time. If you subtract the beginning time from this time, you have 2.69 seconds, as compared to 8.46 seconds with the 8088 CPU.

I then ran a screen from a CAD program that gradually filled the whole screen. Using a stopwatch, I measured 47.53 seconds with the 8088 CPU.

Fig. 3-18. The Breakthru 286 mounted for bench tests.

With the Breakthru installed, it took 14.80 seconds. This is more than three times faster. This was the extent of my benchmark tests, but everything that I ran was two to four times faster. It was a pleasure. Practically, a difference of 47.53 seconds to 14.80 seconds might not seem like much, but if you sit in front of your computer for very long and have to wait a half minute quite often, it can add up to hours of wasted time.

I did have some problems, though. I found that some of my older programs would not run at high speed; the program would hang up and I usually had to shut off the power to reboot.

I also found that it would not let me use my favorite backup software, FASTBACK. I could back up any of the files on the hard disk with FASTBACK, but when I tried to RESTORE those files, it would hang up. To RESTORE, I had to remove the Breakthru and re-install the 8088.

I have not had any experience with the Breakthru 286-12 running at 12 MHz, but the April 27, 1987 issue of *InfoWorld* magazine gave it a very good review. They claimed that this Breakthru was 333 percent faster than the 8088.

There are several other 80286 boards that can speed up your old PC or XT. *InfoWorld* compared several others to the $595 Breakthru 286-12. Two that were compared were the Univation Dream Board, which gave 131 percent increased speed at $512, and the Orchid PC-Turbo 286e, which gave a 321 percent increase at $1,195. The review stated that in some tests, the Orchid had better performance than the Breakthru. This was because Orchid has its own very fast memory on board. The Breakthru relies on the systems memory, which can slow it down if the RAM chips are 150 ns or slower.

Another option is from SOTA (for "State of the Art"). They manufacture a plug-in board (Fig. 3-19) that they call the MotherCard. It has an 80286 CPU that runs at 8 or 10 MHz. It comes with a real-time clock, one megabyte of memory, an optional 80287 coprocessor and an optional "daughter" board for additional memory up to 16 megabytes. Its list price is $995.

Here are the addresses of the companies mentioned above:

Breakthru 286 $395 & $595
PC Support Group
11035 Harry Hines Blvd. #207
Dallas, TX 75229
(214) 351-0564

Univation Dream Board $512
Univation Co.
1037 N. Fairoaks Ave.
Sunnyvale, CA 94089
(408) 745-0180

Orchid PC-Turbo 286e $1195
Orchid Technology
47790 Westinghouse Dr.
Fremont, CA 94536
(415) 490-8586

Mothercard $995
SOTA Technology
657 N. Pastoria
Sunnyvale, CA 94086
(408) 245-3366

Fig. 3-19. The MotherCard from SOTA. (Photo courtesy of SOTA Corp.)

One of the unusual things about PC Support Group (PCSG), the company that makes the Breakthru, is that they will allow you to use it for 60 days, then if you are not satisfied, you can return it. That is exactly what I did. I ordered it strictly for evaluation on an XT. I use an AT most of the time, so I did not really need the Breakthru. After 45 days, I returned it for credit.

The prices quoted above will probably change by the time you read this. These prices were listed for purposes of comparison only. Check with your vendor before ordering any advertised component.

You should be aware that none of these boards will give you all of the power and benefits that are possible with a true AT. These plug-in boards do not provide a 16-bit data bus, so there are many AT-type boards that cannot be used with these systems.

If you can find one at a reasonable price, you might be better off if you buy a Baby AT mother board and use it to replace your PC or XT mother board. Again, the prices of the Baby AT mother boards can vary considerably, from $350 up to $900. By all means, do some comparison shopping.

SPEEDING UP AN AT

When IBM introduced the PC-AT, it was set to operate at 6 MHz, but many people discovered they could replace the 12-MHz crystal with a 16-MHz crystal and increase the speed to 8 MHz. Unlike the PC and the XT, the AT comes with two separate crystals. It is a very simple matter to change the one that controls the clock speed. Almost all of the clone ATs came with three crystals and a switch so the frequency could be changed from 6 MHz (which was divided down from a 12-MHz crystal) to 8 MHz (from a 16-MHz crystal). This option was provided because some of the older software programs, mostly games, would not run properly at 8 MHz. Many of the newer ATs now operate at 10 MHz and some go as high as 12 MHz. Some companies have promised new ATs that will run at 16 MHz.

MOVING UP TO THE 80386

Quadram has developed an 80386 accelerator board for the PC or XT. Intel has also promised to develop one shortly. Their Quad386 XT board runs at 16 MHz, has one megabyte of memory on board and sells for about $1,500. Quadram's address is:

Quadram
One Quad Way
Norcross, GA 30093-2919
(404) 564-5566

Several companies are now manufacturing 80386 accelerator boards for the AT. But again, accelerator boards cannot give you the benefits of having a mother board with the 32-bit bus and other options.

Several companies have announced that they are developing a Baby 80386 mother board that will fit in the PC or XT case. They will probably be on the market by the time you read this. If so, they will be reviewed in most of the computer magazines. If you are trying to learn as much as you can about computers, you should be subscribing to several of the computer magazines listed in Chapter 14.

4

Power Supplies

A computer must have power to operate. But you might not be aware of what happens to the "juice" after it flows through the plug and into your computer.

The electricity that comes out of the wall socket is 110 volts ac, (alternating current). The various integrated circuits and components in the computer require dc, or direct current, at common potentials of +5 volts, −5 volts, +12 volts, and −12 volts. It is the function of the power supply to convert the 110 volts ac into the required dc voltages.

The power supply sits in the right rear corner of the computer. See Fig. 4-1. It has four separate cables with connectors for disk drives. Each of the four cables has four leads. There are two other cables, usually marked P8 and P9, that plug into the mother board. The pin numbers and functions are listed in Chapter 15.

HOW POWER SUPPLIES WORK

Up until a few years ago, most power supplies required a line transformer. The greater the power that had to be supplied, the larger and heavier the line power transformer. A transformer is made of two coils of insulated wire wound on a special iron core. These coils are known as the primary and secondary windings. When the primary winding is hooked up to the 110 volts ac, the alternating current induces an alternating

Fig. 4-1. Inside a switching power supply.

magnetic flux, which has its greatest magnitude when the current level passes through zero. This swinging magnetic flux induces an alternating voltage across the secondary winding of the transformer.

The voltage induced across the secondary winding will be proportional to the ratio of the number of turns in the primary winding to the number of turns in the secondary winding. For instance, if there are 100 turns on the primary winding and 10 on the secondary, and 100 volts is applied to the primary, then 10 volts will appear across the secondary winding.

Wattage is calculated by multiplying the voltage by the amount of current, or amperage. If you draw 10 amps at 12 volts, that would be 12×10 amps $= 120$ watts.

Power supplies must be able to handle the maximum wattage that will be drawn from them. If you try to draw more power than the supply was designed for, the transformer and other components will get hot and can burn up or short out.

The original IBM PC power supply was rated at only 63 watts. That was sufficient because the PC had only five slots and no provision for a hard disk drive. The wattage for the XT supply was more than doubled to 130 watts because of the extra three slots and the hard disk capability. Even this wattage was marginal in some instances, so most of the clone manufacturers upped the capacity to 150 watts.

The PC-AT came out with a 190-watt supply. This was also marginal in some instances, so most of the clone manufacturers now build AT supplies capable of 200 to 220 watts.

The new IBM PS/2 machines have much smaller power supplies because of the extensive use of low-power CMOS, VLSI chips and surface mount technology. For the same reasons, a 150-watt supply is sufficient for the Baby AT systems.

LINE FREQUENCY

One factor that affects the power (amount of wattage) that can pass through a transformer is its ac frequency. For some reason, in the early days of our electrical system, 60 cycles per second (or 60 Hertz), was chosen. We would be a lot better off had they chosen a higher frequency. Electric motors, appliances and many electronic items could be much smaller and more efficient. A motor that is designed to operate at 400 Hz can be about one fourth the size of one that yields the same horsepower at 60 Hz.

INCREASING LINE FREQUENCY

Over the last few years, high-voltage power transistors have been developed. This has made it possible to change the frequency of the input voltage to our power supplies from 60 Hz to as high as 50 kHz.

To increase the line frequency, first make direct current out of the 110 Vac line voltage. This is done by passing it through rectifiers or diodes. The dc voltage is then "chopped up" at a frequency of 20,000 to 50,000 Hertz (Hz) by high-voltage power transistors. This high-frequency voltage is then applied to a small transformer to bring it down to the required low voltages. These low voltages are again rectified into the dc voltages the computer circuits can use.

With this high frequency, an entire 150-watt switching power supply weighs less than the transformer alone would weigh in a 60 Hz system.

Because the high voltage in the power supply can be dangerous, it is built inside a metal box. The metal box also acts as a shield to prevent static and interference due to the chopping circuits. Figure 4-1 shows the inside of a power supply.

REGULATED VOLTAGES

Some of the computer circuits are sensitive and require a very stable, or *regulated*, voltage. If you put a heavy load on an unregulated supply line, drawing more current than normal, the voltage will go down. If you have two boards in your system using 5 volts at 2 amps, and then you add two more boards to draw 4 amps, the voltage will drop considerably.

A regulated supply is designed so that it can supply the extra current at the same voltage if the load is increased or decreased. It is similar to a cruise control on an automobile. You can set the speed you want and it will remain fairly constant going uphill or downhill because the cruise control feeds the engine more or less gasoline as necessary to maintain a constant speed.

FANS

Ordinarily, there should be no sound from the electronic circuits in your computer. Those little electrons are very quiet as they go speeding around inside the silicon chips. The sounds you hear are from the cooling fan in the power supply and the motors of the disk drives.

Heat is the enemy of electronic components. The purpose of the fan that is mounted in the power supply is to draw air through the grill on the front of the computer, pass it over the mother board and the plug-in boards, then down through the power supply and out the back through the screen of the power supply. It is important that nothing is placed in front of the grill of the computer that would block the air. It is also important that there is space enough behind the computer so that the air can pass out freely. If you have any slots that are not being used, the openings in the back of the case should have blank covers installed so that the air will be forced out through the power supply.

SURGE SUPPRESSION

I mentioned earlier, in Chapter 2, the importance of having a power strip with five or six outlets. I also stressed the importance of making sure that it was plugged in properly.

Most power outlet strips claim to have built-in surge protection, but if you only paid $10 to $15 for the strip, it probably only has a couple of ceramic capacitors. These capacitors will provide very little surge protection. True surge protection requires filter circuits that will include several electronic components such as coils, capacitors, and metal oxide varistors.

When your refrigerator kicks on or when any other heavy inductive load is placed on the line, the voltage can at first drop; then high voltage spikes can be fed back into the line. These spikes can cause some problems if they are not filtered out. If you live in an area where there are lightning storms, then you should definitely have a good surge protection system. A good system might cost from $40 up to $130. See Fig. 4-2.

Fig. 4-2. A power outlet strip with surge suppression. (Photo courtesy of Brooks Power Systems).

There are several companies who manufacture outlets with good surge protection. Here are the names and addresses of three:

Dynatech
2744 Scotts Valley Dr.
Scotts Valley, CA 95066
1-800-638-9098

Brooks Power Systems
3569 Bristol Pike, Suite 102
Bensalem, PA 19020
1-800-523-1551

Tripp-Lite
500 N. Orleans
Chicago, IL 60610
(312) 329-1777

POWER INTERRUPTIONS

Usually, when you are working on a computer, the data and whatever you are doing to it is stored in RAM (random access memory). If the power is interrupted, even for an instant, all of the data in memory is lost. A power interruption can occur at any time, usually at the most inopportune moment. Your data should be saved to disk ever 10 or 15 minutes. It usually takes only a few seconds to save your data and resume, but could take several hours to recover or redo a long file if there is a power interruption.

POWER BACKUP

Backup power supplies can take over in the event of a power outage and provide emergency power. Several systems are on the market; one example is shown in Fig. 4-3. Some provide power for only a few minutes—just enough time to allow you to save your data to disk. Others may provide power up to two or more hours.

These power backups cost from $200 to more than $2000, depending on the wattage, number of outlets, amount of regulation surge suppression, and several other factors.

These units usually have a rechargeable battery that is constantly charged by the line current. In the event of a power outage, a power transistor circuit takes over, chops up the dc voltage from the battery, puts it through a step-up transformer to supply 120 volts of alternating current to the computer's power supply. As explained earlier, the switching power supply then transforms the voltage down to the values required by the computer circuits. There are substantial losses each time the voltage is inverted, converted and sent through a transformer. This type of system is not very efficient and can only provide an output for a short time unless you have a very large battery.

The Applied Research and Technology Company of Atlanta has developed a system they call the Continuous Parallel-power System (CPS). Their system has a battery that is charged up by the line, similarly to those described above. However, their system takes the 5- and 12-volt outputs from the battery and connects it in parallel with the output of the computer's power supply. Their cable has a T on the end of it so that it can be plugged into the mother board. The computer power is plugged into the top of the T connector. This connector also supplies power to the disk drives. Their system eliminates the need to invert, convert and transform the voltages, so it is very efficient. It can boot up and provide power for an AT for up to two hours.

Some other systems require a few milliseconds for the backup power to take over. It is possible to lose some data during the switch over. Since

Fig. 4-3. A backup power supply (Photo courtesy Liebert Corporation).

the Applied Research and Technology CPS system applies voltage and current at all times, there is no delay if there is a power outage. It also provides the proper voltage in the event of a "brown-out," in which the voltage falls to a very low level. See Fig. 4-4.

I am fortunate in the San Francisco Bay area in that we seldom ever have any lightning. We occasionally have winter storms that cause power outages. I seldom work on anything on my computer that would justify adding a backup supply.

If you live in an area where there are frequent storms and power outages, and you are working with critical data, then it might be well worthwhile to invest in a backup power system.

Here are the names and addresses of just a few companies that supply backup power systems:

Applied Research and Technology
6400 Powers Ferry Rd., #110
Atlanta, GA 30339
(404) 951-9556

Liebert Corporation
P.O. Box 29186
Columbus, OH 43229
(513) 439-4800

Elgar Corporation
9250 Brown Deer Rd.
San Diego, CA 92121
(800) 854-2213

Computer Power Inc.
124 W. Main St.
High Bridge, NJ 08829
1-800-526-5088

Fig. 4-4. A continuous backup power supply. It is connected in parallel with the computer's power supply and immediately takes over in case of power failure. (Photo courtesy of Applied Research and Technology.)

Tripp-Lite
500 N. Orleans
Chicago, IL 60610
(312) 329-1777

C-Cor Electronics
6150 Lusk Blvd., Floor B-200
San Diego, CA 92121
(800) 445-9366

Sola
1717 Busse Rd.
Elk Grove, IL 60007
(312) 439-2800

ON-BOARD BATTERY BACKUP

Some of the newer CMOS integrated circuits draw very little power. The clock circuits available today are powered by a lithium battery that can last up to ten years.

Most of the present memory circuit ICs still require a fairly large amount of power, but technology is advancing every day. It is probable that in the very near future, there will be CMOS-type memory circuits that can be backed up with a small on-board battery.

There are several powerful laptop and portable units at the present time that are battery operated. There is no reason why the same technology could not be used with desktop units.

5

Floppy Disk Drives

IBM has created a new 3½-inch floppy disk standard with the introduction
of the PS/2 systems. The new disks will store two to four times as much
data in a smaller space.

There are going to be some problems with the new standard. For
one thing, most software vendors supply their programs on 5¼-inch disks.
They are gearing up to offer both sizes, but it will be some time before
all companies can do it. Figure 5-1 shows a 5¼-inch disk alongside a 3½-
inch floppy. Special extender frames fit around the 3½-inch drives and
allow them to be mounted in the standard 5¼-inch slots of the PC, XT
or AT.

There are at least 10 million 5¼-inch disk drives installed in present
systems. Individuals and businesses have billions of 5¼-inch disks with
files and data on them. I have about 500 disks full of files and backups.
IBM has a fairly low-cost software program for copying data from the
5¼-inch to the 3½-inch format. If you don't have a 5¼-inch drive, they
will sell you an external one for about $400.

Eventually, I will install a 3½-inch drive in my system. But I will also
keep my 5¼-inch drive because I am not sure that I will ever have the
time to copy all my present disks to the smaller size. I suspect that many
other individuals and businesses will do the same.

One other reason that the 5¼-inch disks will be around for awhile
is that they are so inexpensive. Some companies are selling them for as

Fig. 5-1. A floppy disk that has been opened up. Marks on disk represent tracks and sectors.

little as 25 cents apiece. The 3½-inch disks cost from $1.50 for standard density up to $15.00 per disk for high density.

Another reason the 5¼-inch disk format will be around for awhile is that the drives are also inexpensive. I have bought new drives (that were perfectly good) for $50 each. Of course, some brand-name drives still cost as much as $150, but I am not convinced they are proportionately better than the low-cost units.

HOW FLOPPY DISK DRIVES OPERATE

The operation of the 3½-inch and the 5¼-inch systems are basically the same. The floppy drive spins a disk much like a record player spins a record. The floppy disk is made from a type of plastic that is coated with iron oxide. It is very similar to the tape that is used in audio tape recorders. It uses a head, much like the record/playback head in a cassette recorder that records (writes) or plays back (reads) the disk. When the head writes or records on the iron oxide surface, a pulse of electricity causes the head to magnetize that portion of track beneath the head. A spot on the track that is magnetized can represent a "1," or if the next spot of the same track is not magnetized, it can represent a "0." When the tracks are played back or read, the head detects whether each portion of the track is magnetized or not and outputs a series of 1's and 0's accordingly.

ROTATION SPEED

The speed of the disk drive and the length of time that a pulse is applied is a factor in the amount of data that can be recorded. Most 5¼-inch floppy drives rotate at 300 rpm. The AT high-density 1.2-M drive rotates at 360 rpm and the 3½-inch drives operate at up to 600 rpm. Hard disks rotate at 3600 rpm. The speed is critical and should be closely regulated.

NUMBER OF TRACKS PER INCH

Before a floppy or hard disk can be used, it must be formatted. The format command partitions the disk into tracks and sectors. During formatting, bad sectors and any faults in the thickness or deposition of the iron oxide media will be checked. If a bad sector is found, it will be locked out so that the rest of the disk can still be used. Most floppy disks have no bad sectors. The hard disk surface is much more critical and almost all of them have some imperfections.

The amount of data that can be placed on a disk depends on the format, the number of tracks, the number of sectors on each track and the coercivity of the magnetic medium. The coercivity of the medium is measured in Oersteds (OE). The higher density disks, such as the 1.2 M and the 1.44 M, have cobalt added to the medium to raise the coercivity.

If you look at the head slot, you will see that there is only a little over one inch of usable space on a 5¼-inch disk. On a 360-K disk, 40 tracks can be recorded on each side through the head slots. Each of the 40 tracks is divided into 9 sectors, and 512 bytes can be stored in each sector. (This yields 368640 bytes; actually only 362596 bytes are available. The other 6144 bytes are used by the disk for the FAT and other utilities.)

The high-density 1.2-M 5¼-inch disk uses a high-coercivity medium and formats 15 sectors on each of its 80 tracks per side. This yields 1,228,800 bytes.

Figure 5-1 shows a 5¼-inch disk that has been opened up. Lines have been drawn on the disk to represent tracks and sectors. The track nearest the outer edge is track 0, the one closest to the center is track 39. There is a small hole near the large center hub hole. This small hole indicates the beginning of *sector* number one. A light emitting diode (LED) shines through this hole and is detected by a photodiode beneath the spinning disk.

The 3½-inch disk has a little less than a one-inch opening for the head slots, but it records 80 tracks on each side. The format of the standard density 3½-inch disk divides each of the 80 tracks into 9 sectors with 512 bytes in each sector. Since it has twice the number of tracks that the 360-K disk has, the amount of data that can be stored on the standard 3½-inch disk is doubled to 720 K.

The high-density 3½-inch disks used on the new IBM PS/2 Models 50, 60 and 80 will also be formatted to 80 tracks on each side, but each track will be divided into 18 sectors with 512 bytes in each sector. Doubling the number of sectors allows 1.44 M to be stored on a single disk.

Eventually, this high-density 3½-inch format will be the standard throughout the industry. Several companies are now making the smaller drives. It is probable that most computers sold in the next few months will have both 3½- and 5¼-inch drives.

There is at least one company, the Manzana Company, who is manufacturing 3½-inch drives that will format to 1.44 M. These drives can be mounted in a PC, XT or an 80286 computer and will be compatible with the PS/2 Models 50, 60 and 80 disks.

HEADS

Many of the early disk drives had only a single head and recorded on one side of the disk only. Most all of the drives today have two heads, one for each side of the floppy disk. Both heads are controlled by a single positioner. If track 1 is being read on the top side, the bottom head is over track 1 on the bottom side. The positioner moves the heads to whatever track or sector that needs to be written to or read from.

CYLINDERS

If you could strip all the other tracks away from track 1 on the top and bottom of the disk, it could be likened to a cylinder. It is very easy and fast to electronically switch from the head on the top at track 1 to the head on the bottom at track 1. When a file is written, track 1 will be written on the top side, then the drive will switch sides, so that the file will continue to be written on track 1 on the bottom side. DOS calls the top side "0," and the bottom side "1." The standard 360-K disk has 40 tracks on each side, so it has 40 cylinders. The 3½-inch 80-track disks have 80 cylinders.

CLUSTERS

Since 512 bytes is rather small, DOS treats two sectors on a track as a single unit and calls it a *cluster*. For instance, if a 3 kilobyte file is recorded on a floppy disk, 1024 bytes might be written in sectors 0 and 1 of track 1. If the next cluster, sectors 2 and 3 of track 1, already has data in it, the next 1024 bytes will be sent to the first available open cluster, which might be on track 20. The directory of the disk has a File

Application Table, or FAT, that keeps track of where each part of the file is placed. This system allows you to add onto an existing file by placing the additional data in any empty cluster. You may also delete any part of a file by erasing one or more clusters.

Two different files or parts of two different files cannot be written in the same cluster. A 1-K file will require one whole cluster of 1024 bytes. If a file had only two bytes it would also require a whole cluster of 1024 bytes of its own. If a file has between 1025 bytes and 2048 bytes, it will require two clusters.

3½-INCH INCH DRIVES

Laptops and some of the Apple products have been using 3½-inch floppy drives for some time. Several companies are making them, so the competition has forced the prices down to a range from $100 up to $150.

DOS 3.2 allows the use of 3½-inch floppies. The standard format is 720 K, but some companies are already manufacturing 3½-inch drives that will format to 1.44 M. Special device drivers will be necessary to format these drives to 1.44 M. Because they are new and there is no competition yet, the cost of the 1.44-M drive is still over $300, but this price will come down very soon.

VERY HIGH DENSITY FLOPPY DRIVES

Kodak, Konica, 3M and several Japanese companies are now manufacturing very high density 5¼-inch drives. These drives can format a disk with several densities from 3.3 M up to 12 M. Most of the drives can read the lower density formats of 1.2 M and 360 K.

Some of the Kodak drives use standard 5¼-inch 600 Oersted disks, which are relatively inexpensive. The Kodak 12-M floppy disk actually formats to 9.9 M. It is encased in a hard shell and has a protective sliding door much like the shell of the 3½-inch disk. This disk is fairly expensive at about $50 each. Figure 5-2 shows an IBM Model 30 with an external Kodak 6-M floppy disk drive attached to it. Figure 5-3 shows an IBM XT with a Kodak 12-M floppy disk drive mounted in it. Notice that the 12-M disk on the left has a hard-shell type cover, much like those on the 3½-inch disks. The prices of the Kodak high density floppy disk drives range from $600 to $1200.

THE BERNOULLI BOX

The IOMEGA Company has a high-density floppy disk that can store up to 20 M on a removable cartridge. On most floppy systems the head

Fig. 5-2. An IBM Model 30 with an external Kodak six-megabyte floppy disk drive.

directly contacts the disk. The heads on the IOMEGA system "fly" microinches above the disk, similarly to the heads on a hard disk. This drive is known as a Bernoulli drive, which refers to the aerodynamic principle allowing such close tolerance. The Bernoulli drive spins at 1820 rpm, approximately half the speed of a hard disk.

The Bernoulli Box is a good system, but it is expensive compared to other alternatives. I have seen ads from some companies who charge $1795 for a 20-megabyte Bernoulli system. They charge $84 for the removable cartridges.

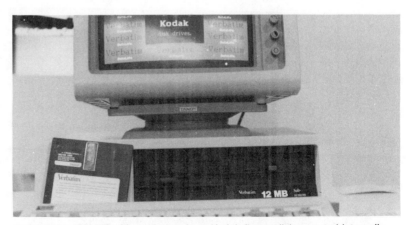

Fig. 5-3. An IBM XT with a 12-megabyte Kodak floppy disk mounted internally.

I have recently seen an ad from the Leading Edge Company for a complete computer system, including a monochrome monitor and a built-in 20-megabyte Bernoulli drive, for only $1995. The Leading Edge Company is selling the 20-megabyte cartridges for $49.95. It definitely pays to shop around and compare prices.

KONICA

Figure 5-4 shows the Konica floppy disk drive. The Konica drive uses a 600 OE disk that is similar to those used on 1.2-M drives, but it formats to 480 tracks per inch, and 10.9 megabytes of data can be stored on one disk. A servo signal is embedded on each track of the disk at the factory. This servo data is then used in a closed-loop system to position the heads over the very narrow tracks. The disks sell for about $18 each.

The drive rotates at 600 rpm rather than the 300 rpm of the standard 360-K drives. The higher rotation speed contributes to the higher recording density. The drive has a built-in Small Computer Systems Interface (SCSI) and controller. It can be plugged directly into the Macintosh, but an adapter card must be used on the IBM and compatible computers. The drive will

Fig. 5-4. A Konica 10-megabyte floppy drive and disks.

sell in original equipment manufacturer (OEM) quantities for about $400. Of course you, the end user, will have to pay more.

This appears to be excellent technology. Had it not been for the introduction of the IBM 3½-inch, 1.44-M floppy, this 10-megabyte 5¼-inch drive might well have been the new standard. Even if it does not become a standard, it has many great advantages and will be quite useful to many users.

ADVANTAGES

The high density disks and removable cartridges have several advantages over hard disks. You always have to worry about a hard disk crashing and destroying all of your files. You might also be concerned about the security of confidential or crucial data.

In most large offices, several people use the same computer from time to time. It is very easy for someone to accidentally erase or alter an important file. Unauthorized copies of files and software might also be made. It is difficult to guarantee the security and integrity of data on a hard disk in a situation like this, but a high capacity floppy or cartridge can be removed and locked up in a secure area. Data stored in this way is also more portable. A program can be developed on one computer, then the disk or cartridge can be moved to another computer in the same room or across the country.

Many software programs (such as Lotus 1-2-3) are copy protected. This allows only one installation on a hard disk. If you want to use such software on another computer, it must be "uninstalled" back onto the original master disk and then installed on another computer.

Even if the software is not copy protected, most license agreements state that the software may be used on only one computer at any time. If there are three or four computers in an office area with hard disks, each one should have a separate copy of any software installed on it.

A person doesn't often use all of the programs on a hard disk in one session. If a person is using a computer to do something like word processing, none of the other programs on the hard disk can be used by anyone else. Expensive programs could be idle much of the time.

This translates to a considerable cost. Unless all of the computers were using the same software at the same time, it might be less expensive to install high density drives on each computer. Then, install each program on a separate high density removable disk so that it can be used on any computer at any time.

A hard disk should be backed up regularly. You can use standard 360-K floppy disks to back up a hard disk, as many as 30 floppies could be required just to back up 10 megabytes. This type of backup can also require a considerable amount of time. One or two very-high-density disks or removable cartridges can do the job easily and quickly.

POWER AND CONTROLLERS

All 5¼-inch floppy disk drives use the standard four-wire connector from the power supply, but some of the new 3¼-inch drives have miniature connectors for both power and controller lines. Adapter cables are available that can be used to connect the small drives.

The PC and PC-XT had a single board that could control up to four floppy disk drives. A new board was designed for the PC-AT that combined the floppy controller and the hard disk controller onto a single board, freeing up a slot.

When it first came out, the AT combination controller board cost about $250. They have since come down to about $150. The AT uses the standard 8-bit bus that the XT uses, so it is possible to use the separate controllers if you are not worried about using an extra slot. I have seen some floppy controllers for as little as $35.

The IBM PS/2 machines have both floppy and hard disk controllers built-in on the mother board. The Model 30 can read, write, and format a 720-K disk. The Models 50, 60, and 80 can read, write, and format both 720-K and 1.44-M disks.

CARE OF DISKS

The heads actually contact the disk, so there is some wear each time a floppy is read from or written to. Disks can be used several hundred times before they wear out, but you should make backups of your master disks and any others that have very important data.

Each disk has a write-protect notch. When the disk is inserted into the drive slot, a light shines through the open notch and allows the disk to be read from, written to, altered, or erased. If this notch is covered, the disk can be read, but it cannot be written on or erased. If you want to protect your data, it is important that the notch be covered with opaque tape so that no light can get through. Some people have used clear Scotch tape with disastrous results. The hard shell of the 3½-inch disk has a plastic slide that can be moved to cover a write-protect hole.

The first thing you should do when you get a new piece of software is to cover the write-protect notch, then make a backup copy. The master should be put safely away, and you should use the backup copy.

It is very easy to hit the wrong key and write over or erase very important data or an expensive master disk. If the copy becomes damaged, you can always make a new backup from the master.

It is very important that the disk be kept clean. You should be careful not to touch the disk through the open slot, which is the head contact area. Finger prints can destroy data. You should also be careful not to allow any magnetic objects near your disks.

If you are traveling by air, do not allow any disks to be sent through the X-ray machines at the boarding gates. The X-rays will completely erase any data on your disks. You should remove any disks from your carry-on luggage and pass them around the X-ray machine, or, since most stowed luggage is not X-rayed, you could pack them in one of those bags.

There has been a tremendous amount of change in computer technology in the last few years. Floppy disk technology has kept pace through constant improvement.

6

Hard Disks
and Mass Storage

You can buy a computer with just one or two floppy drives and no hard disk, but if you think you don't need a hard disk with your computer, then you have probably never had the pleasure of using one. Once you have used a hard disk, you will never again be happy working on a computer without one. Operating a computer without a hard disk is like paddling a canoe without oars.

You may be able to save a few dollars by not buying a hard disk, but if your time is worth anything at all, and you do any serious computing, you will waste far more time than the cost of a hard disk. Besides, they are really not that expensive.

About three years ago, 10 million seemed like a very large number. IBM sold thousands of PC-XTs with ten-megabyte hard disks. At that time, the hard disk cost from $1500 to $2000 each. If you go to a computer swap meet today, you can find those same ten-megabyte hard disks selling for as litter as $75 each. The reason they are so inexpensive is that most people have found that 10 megabytes is not nearly enough storage. Many people have pulled them out and traded them in for larger units.

One reason that ten-megabytes is not enough storage is because much of today's software requires two megabytes of disk space. Many of the more popular programs are now very user friendly. This means that they have lots of on-screen help and many menus. Programs like dBASE III

Plus and WordStar 4.0 are now very easy to use, but each requires about two megabytes of disk storage. Even DOS 3.2 requires well over 300 K of disk space for all of its commands. If you load in a few of these programs, you won't have much workspace left.

One of the main reasons to have a hard disk is for convenience. I have about 500 floppy disks, but I am not very well organized. I used to spend hours looking for a certain disk, but with *all* of my files on my 60 M hard disk, I can find and load any file in just seconds with a few keystrokes. They are no farther away than the tips of my fingers.

There is an intense feeling of power in knowing that you have several hundred programs at your fingertips that can pop up on your screen within milliseconds. But remember, you still need to keep the floppies as backup just in case something happens to your hard disk.

In many cases, you might never have a need for a lot of the software that you accumulate, but there is some kind of immutable and inflexible law that decrees that if you throw something away you will almost certainly need it the next day.

It is an obvious fact of life that you can never have too much money, too much memory, or too much disk space. There seems to be another law that decrees that the requirements for disk space expand to fill whatever is available. This is especially true if the computer is in an office where several people use it, or if it is used in a multiuser environment or as a server on a local area network (LAN).

Some individuals are constantly downloading software from the bulletin boards or exchanging programs among friends or in users' groups. Software companies are like the automobile business. They constantly come out with updates, and whether they need it or not, many people must have the very latest issue. If you are like myself and those described above, you will find it won't take long to fill up a large hard disk and lots of floppies.

You can see why it is essential to have a hard disk. You can also understand why ten megabytes is not nearly enough nowadays. In some instances, even 20 megabytes is not enough. We are fortunate that there is a lot of competition in the manufacture of hard disks. As with most other computer components, the prices of hard disks continue to decline. You can now buy a 20-megabyte hard disk for about $350. A 30-megabyte drive might cost less than $500.

HOW A HARD DISK OPERATES

Basically, the hard disk is similar to the floppy. It is a spinning disk that has a coating that can be magnetized. The hard disks are also formatted similarly to the floppy, but the 360-K floppy disk has only 40 tracks per inch (TPI). A hard disk can have from 300 to 2400 TPI. The 360-K floppy has nine sectors per track and uses two sectors per cluster. The standard hard disk has 17 sectors per track and may use 4 to 16 or more sectors to form one cluster.

Another major difference is the speed of rotation. A floppy disk rotates at about 300 rpm. A hard disk rotates at 360 rpm. As the disk spins beneath the head, a pulse of current through the head causes the area of the track beneath the head to become magnetized. If this pulse is turned on for a certain amount of time and then turned off for some amount of time, it can represent 1's and 0's. The hard disk spins much faster than a floppy, so the duration of the magnetizing pulses can be much shorter at a much higher frequency. This allows much more data to be recorded in the same amount of space.

Everything that a computer does depends on precise timing. Crystals and oscillators are set up so that certain circuits perform a task at a specific time. These oscillating circuits are usually called clock circuits. The clock frequency for the standard Modified Frequency Modulation (MFM) method of reading and writing to a hard disk is 10 MHz. The track on the spinning disk is moving at a constant speed beneath the head. Blocks of data are written or read during the precise timing of the clock. Since the voltage must go to two states in order to write 1's and 0's, the maximum data transfer rate is only 5 MHz—half the clock frequency.

You have probably seen representations of magnetic lines of force around a magnet. A magnetized spot on a disk track has similar lines of force. To read the data on the disk, the head is positioned over the track and the lines of force from each magnetized area causes a pulse of current to be induced in the head. During a precise block of time, an induced pulse usually represents a 1, where the lack of a pulse represents a 0.

The amount of magnetism that is induced on a disk when it is recorded is very small. It must be small so that it will neither affect other tracks on each side of it, nor, affect the tracks on the other side of the thin disk. Magnetic lines of force decrease as you move away from a magnet by the square of the distance, so it is desirable to have the heads be as close to the disk as possible. In fact, the floppy heads actually contact the disk. This causes some wear, but not very much because the rotation is fairly slow and the plastic disks have a special lubricant and are fairly slippery.

In contrast, the heads of hard disk systems never touch the disk. The fragile heads and disk would be severely damaged if they made contact at 3600 rpm. The heads "fly" over the spinning disk, just microinches above it. The air in the hermetically-sealed case must be filtered and pure because the smallest speck of dust or dirt can cause the head to "crash."

Similarly, surfaces of the hard disk platters must be very smooth. Since the heads are only a few millionths of an inch away from the surface, any unevenness could cause a head crash. The hard disk platters are usually made from aluminum, which is non-magnetic, then lapped to a mirror finish. They are coated or plated with a magnetic material.

The platters also must be very rigid so the close distance between the head and the platter surface is maintained. You should avoid any sudden movement of your computer while the disk is spinning because it could cause the head to crash onto the disk and damage it. Most of the newer hard disk systems automatically move the heads away from the read/write surface when the power is turned off.

Incidentally, another difference between hard and floppy disks is that the floppy spins only when it is needed. Because of its mass, the hard disk takes quite a while to get up to a stable speed, so it begins spinning whenever the computer is turned on and spins until the computer is turned off. This means that it is drawing power all the time. This could cause problems if your system is fully loaded with boards and has a small power supply.

MULTIPLE DISKS

So that more recording surfaces can be crammed into a 5¼-inch disk hardware format, a hard disk system can have more than ten platters. All the platters are stacked on a single shaft with just enough spacing between them for the heads. Each platter has one head for the top surface and one for the bottom. If the system has four platters, then it will have eight heads. All heads are controlled by the same positioner and they will all move as one. If head number one is over track one, sector one, then all other heads will be over track one, sector one on each platter surface.

HEAD POSITIONERS

There are several different types of head positioners. Some use stepper motors that move the heads in discrete steps to position them over a certain track. Some use a worm gear or screw-type shaft that moves the heads in and out. Others use voice-coil technology.

The voice coil of a loud speaker is made up of a coil of wire, wound on a hollow tube attached to the speaker cone. Permanent magnets are placed inside the coil and around the outside. Whenever a current is passed through the coil, it will develop a magnetic field around the coil. Depending on the polarity of the input voltage, this magnetic field will either repeal or attract the permanent magnets.

Some of the better and faster hard disks use voice coil technology with a closed-loop serve control. Many of the larger disks use surface of one of the platters to store track locations. The voice coil then moves the heads quickly and smoothly to the track area. Feedback information from the closed loop positions the head at the exact track.

FORMATTING A HARD DISK

If possible, have your vendor format your hard disk for you. The controller cards are usually designed so that they will operate with several different types of hard disks. Most have DIP switches that must be set to configure your particular hard disk. There is usually some documentation that comes with the hard disk controller, but in most cases it is very diffi-cult to understand, especially if you are a beginner.

(One of the points that IBM stresses about their PS/2 systems is that the new Micro Channel will not require DIP switches on the plug-in boards. Each board will come with a unique ID and software on a disk that will be fed into the computer system so that the plug-in board will be automatically configured. Several manufacturers who want to develop boards for the PS/2 have complained that IBM has been very slow in giving them the unique ID number that must be used. IBM has said that if the same ID number is used on two different cards, it will cause problems in the computer.)

The AT controller can control 360-K floppy drives, a 1.2-M floppy drive, and one or two hard disks. There are several controller board manufacturers. The documentation that I have seen for setting up the disks is usually very poor. So again, if at all possible, have your vendor format the disk for you.

You might not understand why it is necessary to format a floppy disk or hard disk. Formatting organizes the disk so that data can be stored and accessed easily and quickly. A brief analogy would be similar to that of a land developer. He would lay out the streets and create blocks. He would then partition each block into lots and build a house on each lot. Each house would have a unique address. A map of these streets and house addresses would be filed with the city.

When a disk is formatted, the tracks and sectors are laid out and a map is filed. This disk map is called the File Application Table, or FAT. Each time data is recorded on a disk, the location of that data is recorded in the FAT. When a disk has been used for some time and files have been recorded, updated, erased, and recorded over again, parts of some files could be located in several areas on the disk. A file will be recorded in the first empty sector, or sectors if it is longer than 512 bytes. For example, if there is an empty sector on track 5, the drive will record as much as it can there, then move to the next empty sector, which might be on track 20. The location of each part of the file is recorded in the FAT.

Again, most standard hard disk systems use the Modified Frequency Modulation (MFM) method. With this system, each track on the disk surface is formatted into 17 sectors, and 512 bytes can be stored in each sector. Therefore, if you multiply 512 bytes by 17 sectors, a total of 8704 bytes can be stored on each track. A typical ten-megabyte hard disk has 306 tracks on each side of its two platters for a total of 1224 tracks. This yields 10,653,696 bytes. If you do a CHKDSK command on one of these disks, you might only see 10,592,256 bytes because 61,440 bytes have been used for the FAT, the directory, and other utilities.

RLL CONTROLLERS

The RLL system was developed by IBM some time ago for use on large mainframe hard disks. A couple of years ago, Adaptec of Milpitas adapted the technology so that it could be used on PC hard disk controllers. Since that time, Scientific Micro Systems of Mt. View and Western Digital have developed similar controllers. Scientific Micro Systems calls their controllers OMTI. Their controller is built on a half card. The original Adaptec 2070A is a full size card, but they also have a half card version, the 2071.

The main difference between the RLL and the MFM systems is that the RLL system manages to squeeze more sectors onto each track. Each sector still has only 512 bytes, but instead of the MFM's 17 sectors per track, the Adaptec RLL has 25 sectors per track and the OMTI has 26. See Fig. 6-1.

Before I retired from Lockheed, I had two XTs with ten-megabyte hard disks. They were always filled to the limit. Every time I wanted to

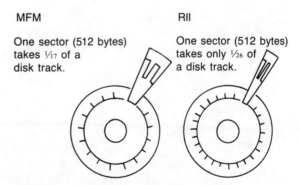

MFM

One sector (512 bytes) takes 1/17 of a disk track.

RII

One sector (512 bytes) takes only 1/26 of a disk track.

Fig. 6-1. Representation of 17 sectors per track using MFM and 26 sectors per track using RLL. (Diagram courtesy Scientific Micro Systems).

use one I had to erase some files to clear a little space, so I talked my boss into letting me install RLL controllers on them.

The controller came with two sheets of instructions for configuring the board for the particular type of hard disk drive and/or reformatting the disk.

LOW-LEVEL FORMAT

The first step in formatting any hard disk is a low-level format, which must be done using the DOS debug command. If you have never done a low-level format, it can be a bit confusing. The instructions might seem rather simple and straightforward, but Bill Boutin of Paramount volunteered to format the disk for me.

I used a copy of FASTBACK to copy all of my files off the hard disk. It took me 9 minutes and 23 seconds to copy 9,924,608 bytes onto 22 floppy disks. I then pulled the hard disk out of the computer and took it over to Paramount. It took Bill about 15 minutes to format it.

A CHKDSK that was done before the hard disk was reformatted showed that it had 10,592,256 bytes total disk space. After reformatting with the OMTI controller, which puts 26 sectors on each track, it showed that there was 16,195,584 bytes of total disk space. Figure 6-2 shows an OMTI half-card RLL controller. It can control two hard disks.

An Adaptec controller was installed on the second ten-megabyte hard disk. Since the Adaptec uses 25 sectors per track, a CHKDSK showed that it had 15,572,992 bytes of total disk space.

At $139 for each controller, I was able to add 50 percent more space on each disk. This is a fantastic way to increase your disk capacity for a relatively low price. Using these controllers, a 20-megabyte disk can

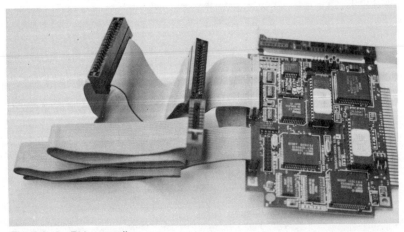

Fig. 6-2. An RLL controller.

give you over 30 megabytes, and a 40 will give 60. Bill Boutin has formatted several 80-megabyte disks to yield 120 megabytes.

Like most standard controllers, the RLL controllers will control two hard disks. The Adaptec controllers can control combinations of 5¼-inch and 3½-inch hard disks or two hard disks of different capacities.

THE 32-MEGABYTE HARD DISK LIMIT

DOS 3.2 has a limit of 32 megabytes that it will address on a hard disk. The 32-megabyte limit is due to the fact that DOS numbers each 512-byte sector sequentially and stores it as a 16-bit integer. Two taken to the 16th power (2^{16}) is 65,536 (or 64 K) of different 16-bit numbers, so DOS can only handle 65,536 sectors. Multiply this number by the 512 bytes in each sector, and you get a total of 33,554,432 bytes or 32 megabytes.

Adaptec controllers allow the use of logical partitioning of large disks. Two large-capacity hard disks can be partitioned into as many as eight logical drives with a total capacity of 256 megabytes using DOS. However, special software is needed for systems using more than 64 megabytes and for logical partitions three through eight.

For these larger drives, Adaptec suggests that you use a software driver that is available from the Ontrack Computer Systems. Ontrack publishes a software package called Disk Manager. It provides the user with the ability to create a custom logical disk structure to meet their specific requirements. It will allow a hard disk to have as many as 16 partitions. It will permit a DOS boot partition of 32 M and a non-bootable partition of as large as 512 M. Their address is:

Ontrack Computer Systems
6222 Bury Dr.
Eden Prairie, MN 55344
(800) 752-1333

IBM has released a 3.3 version of DOS. It adds a couple of features to the 3.2 version. One feature supposedly allows you to overcome the 32-megabyte limitation for hard drives. There have been reports that some people have had some trouble when using 3.3 with some of the clones. However, IBM developed it for their machines only, so they will not accept any responsibility if it does not operate properly on a clone.

RLL is a fantastic and relatively inexpensive way to increase a hard disk's capacity, but some of the older hard disks will not work with these controllers. Adaptec has tested many drives and has found that most of the newer drives that use the thin film-plated and sputtered media will work with the RLL controllers. Many of the older drives that use oxide media and older electronics technology will not work.

The MFM encoding used on ST506/412 drives has a transfer rate of 5 megabits per second with a 100-nanosecond data window. The RLL controllers operate at a transfer rate of 7.5 megabits per second with a 66.6-nanosecond data window. In order to use the RLL controller, the disk drive and its electronics must be able to meet the higher and tighter specifications.

Most of the newer drives will meet these specifications. Most manufacturers are adding "R" after the model number to indicate that it is capable of RLL. Both Scientific Micro Systems and Adaptec have published a fairly long list of the drives they have tested. They are continually testing drives and updating their lists. If your drive is one that is not on the list below, they suggest that you contact your drive vendor before buying an RLL controller.

Drives RLL-Tested by Adaptec and Scientific Micro Systems:

Atasi	3085		V185
			514
Lapine	LT300		519
	TITAN		
		Rodime	RO352
Microscience	HH-325		RO202E
	HH-330		RO203E
	HH-738		RO204E
Micro Storage	MS212	Seagate	ST238
			ST251R
Miniscribe	3425		ST277R
	3438		ST4077R
	8438		ST4144R
Mitsubishi	MR522	Syquest	SQ319
			SQ357
NEC	3126		
	5126	Tandon	TM502
			TM755
Okidata	OD526		
	OD540	Toshiba	MK53FB
			MK54FB
Priam	V150		MK56FA
	V170		MK56FB

Tulin	TL226	TL240
	TL326	TL340

Note that Adaptec, Scientific Micro Systems and Western Digital are manufacturers and not retailers. You should contact a computer dealer for these controllers.

Adaptec has put together a comprehensive user manual for their ACB-2070A controller, but most of the retailers do not offer it. You can purchase it from Adaptec for $6. I would recommend it to anyone who wants to install one of these boards but is not familiar with controllers.

This list is not complete; there are many new companies and new drives being introduced every day. Again, check with your dealer before investing in an RLL controller.

HIGH-CAPACITY HARD DISKS

The June 9, 1987 issue of *PC Magazine* had a very comprehensive review of hard disks. They reviewed several high capacity disks that formatted from 70 to 380 megabytes. Most of them were also very expensive. For instance, the list price of a 120-megabyte drive from the IDEAssociates Company was $7995. A 310-megabyte and 60-megabyte backup tape drive from the Emulex Company was only $7,105. The list price for a Priam 130-megabyte drive was $3598. The average list price for 120 to 160 megabytes was about $4000.

The same issue reviewed some drives that formatted from 20 to 70 megabytes. The list prices ranged from $310 for a 21-megabyte Seagate 238 up to $1350 for a 72-megabyte Fujitsu. A 44-megabyte Miniscribe had a list price of $639.

The published list price of most computer components is almost always discounted by many dealers. You can probably find the Miniscribe listed above at one of the discount houses for about $500.

You can buy an RLL controller, for about $140 that will control two hard disks. Then you could buy two 44-megabyte Miniscribe drives for about $1000. With the RLL controller, the two drives would format to 66 megabytes each for a total of 132 megabytes for less than $1200. Compare this to the 130-megabyte Priam above for $3598 or the IDEAssociates 120-megabyte for $7,995.

The *PC Magazine* tests showed that the Priam had disk-access time of 24.98 milliseconds. The Miniscribe access time was 33.62 milliseconds. Several other tests showed that the two were very nearly equal in other respects.

ARLL AND ERLL

There are at least three companies who are now manufacturing Advanced RLL and Enhanced RLL controller. They are Maynard Electronics, Perstor (of Systems and Software) and Adaptec. These controllers format each track of the hard disk for 33 or 34 sectors instead of the standard 17. This doubles the amount of data that can be stored. Many people are a little leery of these new controllers. Some believe that this might be pushing the technology a bit too much. It does require some very close tolerances and specifications. I have not had a chance to personally evaluate any of these drives.

Adaptec offers several ARLL models. Adaptec was the first company to adapt the RLL concept to PCs. They have some very knowledgeable engineers. Again, I have not seen these drives in operation, but they look great from the data on the specification sheets. Figure 6-3 is a photo of one of their ARLL controllers.

Maynard matches their controller with a drive and sells the controller and drive as a system. A 135-megabyte system will cost about $2795, and a 225-megabyte system, about $5595.

Perstor has tested several high-capacity drives with their controller and claims that they work. They are continually testing drives to add to their list. Write to them at the address below for their latest list. It appears from the data sheets that they sent to me that it is a viable system. The controller will cost about $500.

If you need a lot of disk storage and don't have a lot of money, I would suggest that you investigate the RLL and ARLL controllers. Here are some addresses:

Scientific Micro Systems
339 N. Bernardo Ave.
Mountain View, CA 94043
(415) 964-5700

Adaptec, Inc.
580 Cottonwood Dr.
Milpitas, CA 95035
(408) 432-8600

Maynard Electronics
460 E. Semoran Blvd.
Casselberry, FL 32707
(305) 331-6402

Perstor, Systems & Software
7825 E. Redfield Rd.
Scottsdale, AZ
(602) 948-7313

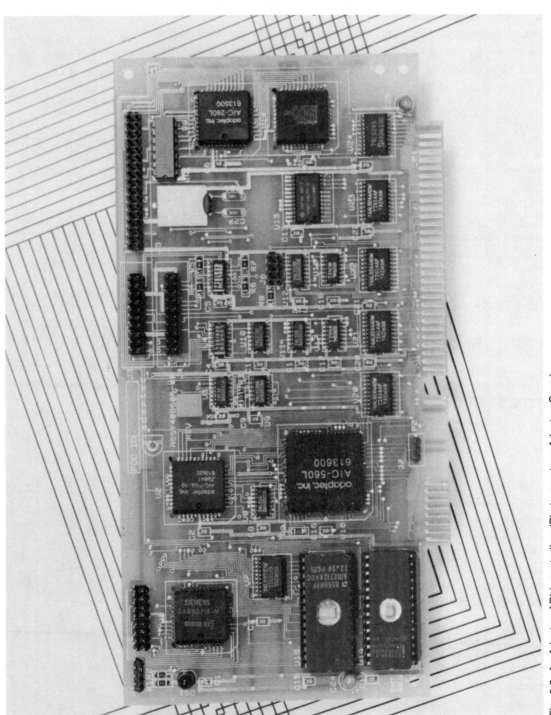

Fig. 6-3. An Adaptec ARLL controller. (Photo courtesy Adaptec Corp.)

THE TRUMP CARD

There are other controllers that pack more data onto a hard disk. One of them is the Konan controller. It uses data compression and compaction to store up to 50 percent more data on a disk. Data compression is not new. In one form or another, it has been a favorite on bulletin boards for several years. (A small public domain software program called Squeeze can squeeze a file down and store it in about half the space ordinarily needed. When you need to run the program, an ''unsqueeze'' command is used to restore it to its original form. There have been several improvements made to the original concept. One of the latest is called Archive.) The Konan controller is on a small half-card. Several companies have used it with small 3½-inch hard drives to make plug-in cards.

The first plug-in hard disk drive on a card was developed by the Quantum Corporation of Milpitas in mid-1985. It was 10 megabytes and could be plugged into an IBM PC, XT, or compatible. There were no cables to worry about, and it was very easy to install and remove. It could be taken out and locked up for security purposes or could be shipped across the country and plugged into another computer. It was a fantastic idea.

It wasn't long before several other companies came out with a plug-in hard card. Most of them had 20 megabytes and sold for about the same as the Quantum hard card. About a year later, some companies came out with 30 megabytes on a card. This seemed to be the absolute limit for hard cards for some time.

However, in November of 1986, Universal Peripherals International Corporation (UPIC) demonstrated hard cards with capacities of 30 M, 45 M and 60 M at the Fall COMDEX. They called them Trumpcards. They have recently demonstrated an 80-M Trumpcard.

All of the models are the same size, use 3½-inch hard drives with a Konan controller, and fit on a standard full-length plug-in card. The drive portion is mounted on the front half of the card and is 1.7 inches thick. This means that the drive portion of the board will extend over the front half of the space of the adjoining slot, but with today's surface mount technology (Very Large Scale Integration or VLSI and Application Specific Integrated Circuits or ASIC), many of today's standard boards have been reduced to short half-boards. A half-board easily fits into the slot next to a Trumpcard, so you can still have use of all your slots. See Fig. 6-4.

The Trumpcards can be used in the IBM PCs, XTs, ATs or compatibles. They can only be installed in one of the two eight-bit slots of the AT because the full width of the board is used for electronics. There is a notch at the end of the edge connectors that allows it to be seated. The extra 36-pin connector of the 16-bit slots would not allow the board to be seated.

Fig. 6-4. A hard disk on a card mounted in an AT.

The hard disks on a card can be used in Local Area Networks as a file server or in any system where a hard disk can be used.

UPIC is able to cram as much as 80 M onto a 3½-inch disk-on-a-card by using selected high-capacity 3½-inch hard disks and the data compression, compaction, and variable cluster sizes that the Konan controller makes possible.

FRAGMENTATION CONTROL

Remember that when data is written onto a disk, the File Allocation Table (FAT) keeps track of where each file is stored. A file will be stored in the first available empty cluster. If it is a long file, portions of it can be recorded in several clusters, which could be anywhere on either side of the disk. If the data on the disk is frequently edited, changed, deleted, or erased, there could be several empty clusters and the data could be scattered out all over the disk. This is called fragmentation. This can severely slow access time, because it takes time for the heads to move to another track where they must stop, settle, and stabilize before they can read the data.

One way to alleviate the problem of fragmentation is to periodically copy all of the files onto a backup tape or floppy disks, erase all the files from the hard disk, then restore the files from the backup. (There are some software programs such as the Mace Utilities that will unfragment and re-organize the data on a hard disk without going through the steps listed above. There are several other utilities on the Mace disk, but if it did nothing but unfragment your disk, it would still be well worth the money.)

The built-in electronics on the Trumpcard automatically reorganize the data and keeps them in contiguous clusters. Since this reorganization takes some time to accomplish, the system waits until it has free time to do it. Since all of the data in each file is in contiguous clusters, it can be accessed very quickly. The Trumpcard also uses a cache system that speeds up both the read and write access time. The larger the cache, the faster the access time; you can determine the size. The cache uses your RAM memory, so if you make the cache too large, you might have problems running some of your memory-hungry programs.

The Trumpcard system also uses a variable Error Correction Coding system that is based on the degree of compression and compaction of each cluster. It is very accurate and can detect and correct errors to a much greater extent than the standard Modified Frequency Modulation (MFM) system. If the Trumpcard finds hard errors on the disk, it will map them out and prevent their use.

The Trumpcard system uses variable length clusters that fit the length of the file, so there is never any empty space in their clusters. See Fig. 6-5.

The form of compression and compaction used on the files is similar to that used by bulletin boards for archiving. The built-in electronics on the Trumpcard controller compress and decompress the data as it is written

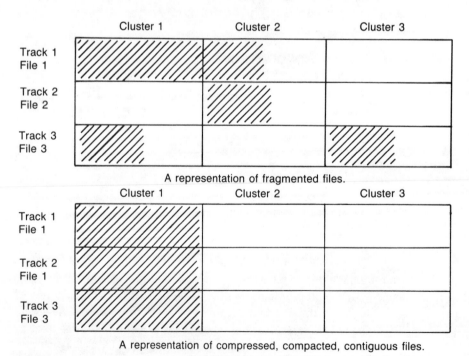

A representation of fragmented files.

A representation of compressed, compacted, contiguous files.

Fig. 6-5. A representation of disk fragmentation and compaction.

on the disk or read back off it. The amount of compression varies with the type of data. Graphics and some repetitive string-type files can be compressed by as much as eight to one. This means that an 80 K file would fit in 10 K of disk space. However, many files can only be compressed by 20 to 30 percent. (A software program called CUBIT can compress and decompress the data written and read from a hard disk, but it slows down the access time considerably). Disk capacity is usually increased by over 50 percent. A standard 20-M hard disk stores about 36 M and a 40-M disk will store over 60 M using the UPIC methods.

The Trumpcard has the built-in capability to overcome the DOS 32-megabyte hard disk limit. They suggest that you partition the disk into a small C: drive and have the rest of it be the D: drive. A floppy disk and an installation manual comes with each Trumpcard. The manual has some very good basic information in it, but it is not needed to install the drive. All that is needed is to put the floppy disk in the A: drive and type {installt}. You are given the option of changing the size of the partition if you want to.

The controller on the Trumpcard is similar to the standard hard disk controllers in that it can control two hard disks. It has connectors for cables to control an internally or externally mounted hard disk. This second hard disk would use the same type of variable length clusters and data compression and compaction that is used on the first disk. It can be almost any kind or size hard disk. It does not have to be mounted on a card.

Steve Cooper, a design engineer for UPIC, says that he has set himself a goal to put over 100 M on a Trumpcard. He says he is convinced he will be able to do so in the very near future. That is almost incredible, but I believe him.

Call or write for their latest models and price list:

Universal Peripherals International Corp.
100 Homeland
Court, Suite 100
San Jose, CA 95112
(408) 947-8742

OTHER HARD CARDS

There are several other companies that make plug-in hard cards. Most of them are still only 20 to 30 megabytes. Rodime has developed a 45-megabyte card by using RLL on a 3½-inch 30-megabyte hard disk. I would expect that several other companies will soon be offering much larger hard disks on a plug-in card. (See Fig. 6-6.)

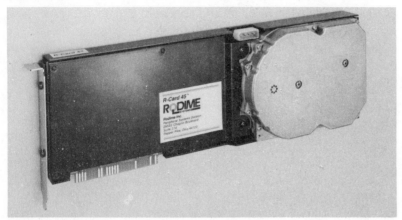

Fig. 6-6. A 45-rnegabyte hard disk on a card. (Photo courtesy Rodime Corp.)

DIAGNOSTIC DISK

When you buy an AT, you should get a diagnostic disk with it. This disk has the routines for checking out and setting up your machine. It is also needed to set or reset the clock on the mother board. The diagnostic routine asks several questions, then configures the BIOS. This part of the BIOS is in low-power CMOS semiconductors and they are powered by a battery pack on the back panel of the computer. The BIOS configuration is on all the time, even when the computer is turned off. If the batteries go too low to power the BIOS, a large capacitor powers it for about 15 minutes (or the time it would take to replace the batteries).

One question the routine asks is what type of hard disk you have. There are 15 different types that the AT supports, but you must tell it what type you have installed. I gave it the wrong type and it cost me a couple of hours and a trip to the dealer. The battery had to be disconnected, and the capacitor needed about 20 minutes to drain off. Only then were we able to reconfigure the system so that the hard disk could be accessed. Incidentally, my 40-megabyte Hitachi, which, with OMTI RLL is now 60 megabytes, is a type "3." I will remember that for a long time.

DISK ACCESS TIME

A very important factor to look for when buying a hard drive is access time. This is the average time it takes to find and read any random byte on the hard disk. The AT specification set by IBM is 40 milliseconds (ms) or less. The XT specification is 85 ms.

INTERLEAVE FACTOR

The XT requirements are slower because the system clock speed of 4.77 MHz cannot handle anything much faster than 85 ms. Even 85 ms is too fast to read the data directly from the hard disk.

I said earlier that the disks are formatted with consecutive sectors on each track. That is not so in most cases, especially for the XT computers. If you want to read the data in sectors 1, 2, and 3 on track 1, the head would be moved over track 1 and sector 1 would be read. By the time our system had transferred sector 1 data to the CPU, the spinning disk would have already spun past sector 2. You can't slow the disk down to wait for the computer, so the CPU must wait for the disk to spin completely around to be able to read sector 2. If you were trying to read a very long file, it could take a considerable amount of time for the data to be read.

Since it takes a finite amount of time to read and absorb the data from a sector, an *interleave* system was devised. Instead of being sequentially formatted, the sectors are enumerated with a few, perhaps four, physically contiguous sectors intervening between sequential sectors. When the end of the track is reached, the formatting is continued in the sectors that were skipped the first time around. Every sequential sector would be four sectors apart.

With this system, the head could read sector 1, and by the time it had passed the next four sectors, the computer would be ready to accept the data from sector 2. This speeds things up because the CPU does not have to wait for the disk to make a complete revolution.

The original PC-XT used an interleave ratio of six to one. The turbo 8-MHz models could usually get by with four to one. The 80286 can get by easily with three to one or less; some can even achieve an even ratio.

The interleave factor may not seem to be important, but it can make a lot of difference if you are reading long files. It must be set when the low-level format is done. In many cases, it is set very conservatively. The only way you can change it, or experiment with different settings, is to do a low-level format on the disk and try it. All data must be backed up before any formatting is done, because formatting erases everything. The formatting itself can take quite a bit of time and requires some expertise.

Steve Gibson of Gibson Research Corporation writes a very interesting column for *InfoWorld* magazine. He has developed a program that will allow you to re-interleave your hard disk for optimum performance without having to reformat your hard disk. He has also developed the following two BA-SIC programs that can be used to test the speed and interleave factor of your hard disk (see Figs. 6-7 and 6-8). Notice that the two programs both use the same statements number 10 through 120. You only need to type those statements in once; then copy them to the second program. (These programs are reprinted with Steve's permission.) If you would like his re-interleave program, or any of his other programs, write to him at:

Gibson Research Corp.
Box 6024
Irvine, CA 92716

```
10 DEFINT A-Z: DIM D(500) : KEY OFF: CLS: PRINT "GIBSON RESEARCH": LOCATE 1,61
20 PRINT "PAPERWARE CONVERTER" : FOR Z =1 TO 80 : PRINT CHR$(205); : NEXT
30 READ F$ : READ FL : LOCATE 4,20 : PRINT "CHECKING THE DATA FOR: ";F$
40 IF X=FL THEN 80 ELSE READ N$ : N=VAL("&H"+N$) : T=T+N : C=C+1
50  IF C<>15 THEN X=X+1 : D(X)=N : GOTO 40
60  IF T MOD 256 THEN PRINT : PRINT "AN ERROR IS PRESENT IN LINE: ";1010+LN :END
70  LN=LN+10 : T=0 : C=0 : GOTO 40
80 PRINT : PRINT "ALL DATA STATEMENTS ARE OKAY! .... NOW CREATING ";F$ : PRINT
90 OPEN F$ AS #1 LEN=1 : FIELD #1,1 AS DT$ : FOR X=1 TO FL :
100 LSET DT$=CHR$(D(X)) : PUT #1 : NEXT : CLOSE ALL
110 PRINT "YOU NOW HAVE THE NEW COMMAND ";F$" IN YOUR DIRECTORY." : SYSTEM
120 '------------------------------------------------------------------'
1000 DATA "SPINTEST.COM", 305
1010 DATA  FC, BC, 31, 0A, BA,  BB, 01, B4, 09, CD,  21, B4, 08, B2, 7E
1020 DATA  80, CD, 13, BA, 21,  02, 72, 52, 80, E1,  3F, 88, 0E, B5, 14
1030 DATA  01, BE, D3, 00, B0,  01, E8, 49, 00, B4,  00, CD, 1A, 52, 9F
1040 DATA  A0, B5, 01, E8, 3E,  00, B4, 00, CD, 1A,  58, 2B, C2, 79, 2B
1050 DATA  02, F7, D8, 01, 06,  B7, 01, 4E, 75, DE,  A1, B7, 01, B1, C5
1060 DATA  06, D3, E8, A3, B7,  01, 33, D2, BF, D6,  01, E8, 38, 00, 29
1070 DATA  A1, B3, 01, F7, 36,  B7, 01, F7, 26, B5,  01, BF, FE, 01, 35
1080 DATA  E8, 27, 00, BA, CC,  01, B4, 09, CD, 21,  CD, 20, B4, 02, 1C
1090 DATA  8C, CB, 81, C3, A4,  10, 81, E3, 00, F0,  8E, C3, 33, DB, FE
1100 DATA  B9, 01, 00, BA, 80,  00, CD, 13, BA, 21,  02, 72, DD, C3, 3D
1110 DATA  B9, 0A, 00, 50, 8B,  C2, 33, D2, F7, F1,  5B, 50, 8B, C3, BA
1120 DATA  F7, F1, 80, C2, 30,  4F, 80, 3D, 2C, 74,  FA, 88, 15, 5A, 09
1130 DATA  83, FA, 00, 75, E2,  3D, 00, 00, 75, DD,  C3, 00, 78, 00, 62
1140 DATA  00, F8, FF, 00, F0,  0D, 0A, 53, 70, 69,  6E, 54, 65, 73, 3C
1150 DATA  74, 69, 6E, 67, 2E,  2E, 2E, 24, 0D, 0A,  0A, 20, 20, 20, 1F
1160 DATA  20, 20, 20, 20, 20,  3A, 20, 72, 65, 76,  6F, 6C, 75, 74, F5
1170 DATA  69, 6F, 6E, 73, 20,  74, 6F, 20, 72, 65,  61, 64, 20, 61, 07
1180 DATA  20, 74, 72, 61, 63,  6B, 2C, 0D, 0A, 20,  20, 20, 2C, 20, DC
1190 DATA  20, 20, 20, 3A, 20,  62, 79, 74, 65, 73,  20, 74, 72, 61, B8
1200 DATA  6E, 73, 66, 65, 72,  72, 65, 64, 20, 70,  65, 72, 20, 73, AD
1210 DATA  65, 63, 6F, 6E, 64,  2E, 0D, 0A, 24, 53,  79, 73, 74, 65, 76
1220 DATA  6D, 20, 45, 72, 72,  6F, 72, 2E, 0D, 0A,  24, 00
```
Fig. 6-7. SPINTEST.

```
10 DEFINT A-Z: DIM D(500) : KEY OFF: CLS: PRINT "GIBSON RESEARCH": LOCATE 1,61
20 PRINT "PAPERWARE CONVERTER" : FOR Z =1 TO 80 : PRINT CHR$(205); : NEXT
30 READ F$ : READ FL : LOCATE 4,20 : PRINT "CHECKING THE DATA FOR: ";F$
40 IF X=FL THEN 80 ELSE READ N$ : N=VAL("&H"+N$) : T=T+N : C=C+1
50  IF C<>15 THEN X=X+1 : D(X)=N : GOTO 40
```
Fig. 6-8. SPINTIME.

```
60  IF T MOD 256 THEN PRINT : PRINT "AN ERROR IS PRESENT IN LINE: ";1010+LN :END
70  LN=LN+10 : T=0 : C=0 : GOTO 40
80  PRINT : PRINT "ALL DATA STATEMENTS ARE OKAY! .... NOW CREATING ";F$ : PRINT
90  OPEN F$ AS #1 LEN=1 : FIELD #1,1 AS DT$ : FOR X=1 TO FL :
100 LSET DT$=CHR$(D(X)) : PUT #1 : NEXT : CLOSE ALL
110 PRINT "YOU NOW HAVE THE NEW COMMAND ";F$" IN YOUR DIRECTORY." : SYSTEM
120 '-------------------------------------------------------------------'
1000 DATA "SPINTIME.COM", 162
1010 DATA FC, BC, A2, 09, BA,   66, 01, B4, 09, CD,   21, E8, 39, 00, B0
1020 DATA B4, 00, CD, 1A, 81,   C2, 44, 04, 8B, F2,   BF, 02, 00, E8, B4
1030 DATA 29, 00, 47, B4, 00,   CD, 1A, 3B, D6, 75,   F4, 8B, C7, B9, 70
1040 DATA 0A, 00, BF, 87, 01,   33, D2, F7, F1, 80,   C2, 30, 4F, 88, 79
1050 DATA 15, 3D, 00, 00, 75,   F1, BA, 82, 01, B4,   09, CD, 21, CD, 93
1060 DATA 20, B8, 01, 02, 8C,   CB, 81, C3, 9B, 10,   81, E3, 00, F0, 8B
1070 DATA 8E, C3, 33, DB, B9,   01, 00, BA, 80, 00,   CD, 13, BA, 92, 81
1080 DATA 01, 72, DC, C3, 0D,   0A, 48, 61, 72, 64,   20, 64, 69, 73, F8
1090 DATA 6B, 20. 73, 70, 69,   6E, 20, 72, 61, 74,   65, 20, 69, 73, F3
1100 DATA 2E, 2E, 2E, 24, 20,   20, 20, 20, 20, 20,   F1, 32, 20, 52, FD
1110 DATA 50, 4D, 2E, 0D, 0A,   24, 53, 79, 73, 74,   65, 6D, 20, 45, 10
1120 DATA 72, 72, 6F, 72, 2E,   0D, 0A, 24, D2,
```

CD-ROM

The Compact Disk Read Only Memory (CD-ROM) industry is one of the fastest growing of all the computer peripheral industries. Sony, Hitachi, Phillips, JVC, Amdek, Panasonic, and several others are manufacturing the drives. These drives are all compatible and can be interfaced to a PC, XT, AT, or compatible with a plug-in board. A couple of years ago, only two or three companies had any material on these disks. The June 1987 issue of *CD-ROM Review Magazine* listed over 100 companies who have disks filled with PC-SIG's public domain software, Grolier's Electronic Encyclopedia, Bowkers Books in Print, and hundreds of other titles.

Microsoft, who developed DOS, recently sponsored a CD-ROM International Conference. Several new products were introduced. One was Microsoft's own release, a disk they call the Bookshelf. It has ten resources to aid writers, including word processing, a dictionary, a thesaurus, a spelling checker, a usage guide, a ZIP code directory, and several other resources.

You could plug in the Grolier's or Knowledgeset's encyclopedia and search through the whole set for a single phrase or subject in just minutes. There are several large research, resource, and data base companies that publish disks.

PC-SIG offers over 20,000 software files on a single CD-ROM. Most of the software is public domain; some is shareware. The disk costs $295, which is less than the cost of some individual commercial software programs. Of course, you will need a drive to play it. The drives might cost from $850 up to $1695.

Many companies need to archive their records. Personnel records, financial and payroll records, and dozens of other important documents need to be kept. Some companies have put these records on microfilm and on tape, but microfilm is difficult to search. Tape is not much easier, because the records are written sequentially and you might have to go through 3000 feet of tape to find a record.

In addition, tape must be protected from strong magnetic fields and kept in a controlled environment. Even then, it will begin to deteriorate in about 10 years.

Many companies have found that it is much easier to store those records on compact disks. They are not nearly as fragile as tape, and any record can be searched for and retrieved in seconds. Another plus is that a roomful of tape can be stored on a single CD-ROM—maybe not a large roomful of tapes, but it can hold several 3600-foot long tapes.

PC-SIG and several other companies now offer a service of transferring company tapes and records to CD-ROM. Some of the companies even use scanners that can read your printed documents and files, convert the text into ASCII, and record it on the CD-ROM. Things like invoices and incoming correspondence could be recorded and stored in the very small space of a 5¼-inch plastic disc. If you wanted to find a certain invoice, it could be searched for, found, and printed out in a short time.

You can be sure that the prices of CD-ROM drives and disks will be coming down as more companies enter the market. Right now, they are an interesting adjunct to the computer, but in a short time they will become a necessity.

WORMS

The Write Once Read Many (WORM) type of laser disks are similar to the CD-ROM, except that CD-ROM is Read Only. The WORM lets you write data with a laser onto a disk. One gigabyte or more can be written on a single disk.

The data can be arranged into the desired form with a computer, stored on a hard disk, then transferred to the WORM laser system. Many have complained that WORMs cannot be erased and changed like a magnetic hard disk, but as stated above, there are certain records that should never be changed. Besides, there is enough space on these disks that an update can be written alongside the original. When a disk is filled, start another. I expect that the cost of the blank disks will eventually be less than $10 each. A WORM would make a great backup medium for all of your software and files. Figure 6-9 shows a Toshiba WORM system and cartridge.

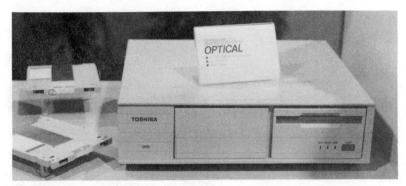

Fig. 6-9. A Toshiba WORM disk system.

BACKUP

Anyone who uses a had disk should periodically back up their files and data. Most hard disks are now relatively bug-free and have a projected Mean Time Before Failure (MTBF) of several thousand hours, but that is only an average. There is no absolute guarantee that your hard disk won't fail in the next few minutes.

There are several backup systems on the market. Tape backup is undoubtedly the easiest method, but it can be relatively expensive, costing $600 to over $1500 for a drive unit and $10 to $30 for each tape cartridge. Most of them use an expansion slot for the controller and, unless used externally, require a mounting area that could house another hard or floppy disk drive. Since the backup drive is only used for backup, it will be idle most of the time. Figure 6-10 shows a backup tape and controller.

A high-density floppy disk drive would be more useful as a backup. Most of the tape drives use the same amount of space to mount the drive as a floppy drive requires. In addition, most of the floppy drives now use the same controller that the hard drive uses. The tape drives are only used once a day or even once a week. The rest of the time they are idle and take up space. A high-density floppy would have much more utility than the tape drive, which can do nothing except backup.

If you have several computers in an office that must be backed up every day, you would install a controller in each machine with an external connector. One external tape drive could then be used to back up each of the computers at the end of the day. With this system, you would need a controller in each machine, but you would only have to buy one tape drive.

There are several very good software programs on the market that let you use an ordinary 5¼-inch or 3½-inch disk drive to back up your data. Ordinarily, you will have backups of all your master software, so you shouldn't have to worry about backing up that software every day. Once you have backed up your files, you need only back up those files

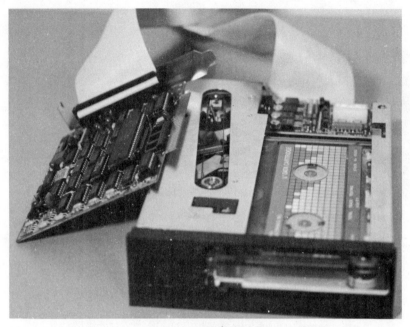

Fig. 6-10. A tape backup drive with cartridge, cable, and controller.

that have changed since the last backup. Since DOS stamps each file with the date and time it was created, it is easy to back up only those files that were created after a certain date and time. (The original PCs and XTs did not come with a clock. Many clone makers jumped at the opportunity to design multifunction boards with clocks. However, all of the AT machines come with a built-in clock. If you do not have a clock, by all means you should buy a multifunction board with one on it. Some companies have devised a clock that fits beneath one of the ROM chips, freeing up an expansion slot.)

Some of the backup software available is Fastback by Fifth Generation and Backit by Gazelle. DOS also has backup and restore commands. The new DOS 3.3 has enhanced the backup and restore commands to make them a little easier than before.

Unless you have a very large amount of data to back up each day, I would suggest that you invest in a high-density floppy drive. It will cost about the same or less than a tape backup, and yet be much more useful.

THE INEVITABLE FAILURE

Hard disk technology has improved tremendously over the last few years, but they are still mechanical devices. And as such, you can be sure that eventually they will fail.

Fig. 6-11. A hard disk that has horribly crashed. (Disk furnished for photo by Rotating Memory Service of Santa Clara).

Fig. 6-12. A hard disk that has been shot three times with a magnum .357. (Drive was furnished for photo by Rotating Memory Service of Santa Clara.)

Quite often most of your data can be recovered after a crash, but a failure can be frustrating and make you feel utterly helpless at times. Figure 6-11 shows a horribly crashed disk. Figure 6-12 shows what one man did when his hard disk failed him. He probably felt a little better after he had pumped three .357 magnum bullets into his hard disk. The disk was brought to Rotating Memory Service, a disk repair service in Santa Clara, but there wasn't much that they could do to recover any data that might have been on the disk.

I know how the person must have felt. I have often felt the same utter frustration. Luckily for my computer, I don't have a gun in the house.

7

Monitors

One of the decisions you must make when you buy your system is what kind of monitor to buy. Many of the ads for computers are quite misleading. Often they will show a complete system with a monitor, but they might not tell you that the monitor is extra until you get down to the store. Even the new IBM PS/2 "M*A*S*H" series of ads shows monitors attached to all of the computers. Of course, IBM doesn't list the prices like the ads of many of the smaller dealers.

There are hundreds of different types and manufacturers of monitors. You have a very wide choice as to price, resolution, color, size, and shape. One can pay as little as $100 for a fairly good monochrome 12-inch monitor, or as much as $10,000 for a super-high-resolution 19-inch color monitor and adapter.

MONITOR BASICS

Basically, a *monitor* (or display device) is similar to a television set. The face of a TV set or a monitor is the end of a Cathode Ray Tube (CRT). CRTs are vacuum tubes that have many of the same elements that made up the old radio and electronic vacuum tubes that were used before the advent of semiconductors. The CRTs have a filament that emits a stream of electrons. These electrons have a potential of about 25,000 volts. They are "shot" from electron guns toward the front of the CRT, where they slam into the phosphor on the back side of the face and cause it to light up.

This stream or beam of electrons must pass between a system of electromagnets before it reaches the back side of the CRT face. In a basic system there would be an electromagnet on the left, one on the right, one at the top, and one at the bottom. Current through the electromagnets can be varied so that the beam of electrons is deflected along two axes.

The CRT also has control grids like those in the old vacuum tubes for controlling the beam intensity. The control grid, along with the electromagnetic system, causes the electron stream to emulate the input signal and write it on the screen.

FLAT SCREENS

If you look closely at your monitor, you will see that it is curved from top to bottom and from side to side. The screen is curved so that the electron beam has the same distance to travel to any area of the face. If the beam takes longer to get to the lower right corner of the screen than to the center of the screen, there will be distortion. With the rounded face, every pixel on the screen is the same distance from the electron gun.

However, the curved screen causes a glare of reflected light that can be very disturbing. Several companies have now devised a way to make a flat screen that has less glare and even less distortion.

SCANNING FREQUENCY

The electromagnets can manipulate the beam of electrons to start writing at the top left corner of the CRT, move all the way across to the top right corner, then move back to the left side and drop down one line and write another line across the screen. It does this very quickly and soon fills the entire screen with 512 lines in about $\frac{1}{60}$th of a second, which is the vertical scan rate. Some of the newer multisync monitors can have variable vertical scan rates from $\frac{1}{40}$th of a second to $\frac{1}{1000}$th of a second in painting the screen from top to bottom.

The horizontal scanning frequency of a standard TV set is 15.75 kHz. Many monitors use the same frequency, but the better ones can have horizontal frequencies from 15.5 kHz to 45 kHz or more.

PERSISTENCE OF VISION

When electrons strike the phosphor, it lights up only briefly, so the beam is brought back to the top left of the screen and each line is written over again, or refreshed. Actually, most of the screen is blank for much of the time, but because of our comparatively slow vision, the screen appears to be lit up all the time.

You can prove this by taking a photo of the screen. Figure 7-1 is the WordStar4 opening menu. The top photo was taken at ⅟₆₀th of a second. The bottom was taken at the much faster rate of ⅟₁₂₅ of a second. Notice that the top part of the screen appears dark. But if you had been watching it you would have not noticed this phenomenon.

RESOLUTION AND PIXELS

If you look at a photo from a newspaper with a magnifying glass, you will see that the picture is made up of dots. Some of the dots are closer together than others, which gives the picture shading and definition. The electron beam creates images in much the same way. As a beam moves across the screen it is turned on and off so that only certain pixels are caused to light up. Unlike printer's ink, intensity of the beam can also be controlled so that an image can be formed with varying shades of gray.

A color system has three electron guns—one each for the red, green and blue (RGB). The monochrome CRT has a single-color phosphor, usually green or amber. Some of the newer monochrome monitors, especially those developed for desktop publishing, are black and white. The text can be black on a white background or vice versa. The color CRT has many small dots of red, green and blue placed close to each other. These three primary colors can be blended to represent any shade or color. The electron beams are directed to the colored dots and cause them to light up with varying intensity to create colors and images.

If you would like to see what the dots look like, take a fairly strong magnifying glass and look at some text or graphics on a color screen. The white letters will have all of the colors lit up. If there is a blue, red, or green on the screen, only that color will be lit. Of course, if an area is black, no pixels will be lit.

Since the monochrome CRTs have only one color phosphor, the pixels (picture cells or dots), are usually very close together. The color monitors have three different dots that must be lit up by beams from three different guns, so the resolution is not as good in standard color monitors as in monochrome monitors. However, there are some good high-resolution color monitors. Naturally, the higher the resolution the higher the cost, because the dots must be smaller and placed closer together. The smaller dots mean that the beams must be more accurately aimed so they will not impinge on adjacent colors. The manufacture of high-resolution monitors demands much closer tolerances. This makes them much more costly than monochrome monitors.

Fig. 7-1. Demonstrating persistence of vision. The photo on top was taken at ⅙₀th second and shows whole screen. The photo on the bottom was taken at the much faster ¹⁄₁₂₅th of a second and shows that top part of screen has gone dark.

DOT PITCH

The color monitor has a perforated mask called a shadow mask. This mask filters the three electron beams so that they strike only their color. The shadow mask must be placed very accurately. If it is not secure, vibrations can cause distortion. As it heats up, the expansion of the material can also cause problems. Several new pre-stressed materials and new installation methods are now being used to reduce these problems.

The spacing between the perforations is called dot pitch. The smaller the spacing, the finer the resolution. A typical medium resolution would be .38 mm. A high-resolution monitor might have a pitch of .31 mm or less; some with very high resolution might have a dot pitch of .26 mm or .24 mm. Some very expensive monitors might have a pitch as low as .21 mm. A Japanese company developed an experimental model with .15 mm dot pitch but it cost about a million dollars to manufacture. I don't think we will be seeing many of those around for awhile, but technology is improving every day.

If you look at the characters or images on a low-resolution monitor, you can see open spaces. A high-resolution monitor will have good, solid, sharply defined letters and images. It is somewhat like the print of a low-cost dot-matrix printer as compared to a good letter-quality one.

MONITORS AND ADAPTERS

You cannot simply plug a monitor into a computer and have it work. It must have an interface. IBM calls the monitor a display and the interfaces are called display adapters.

A whole book could be written about adapters. There are three basic types: the monochrome display adapter (MDA), the color/graphics adapter (CGA), and the enhanced graphics adapter (EGA). Some of the adapters have other built-in functions such as a parallel or a serial port for printers and modems.

The original monochrome monitor with an MDA could display text at a high resolution, but not graphics. Text characters and graphics images are quite different and are handled and stored differently. Monitor controller boards usually have all the alphanumeric characters stored in ROM. When you press A on the keyboard, data for A is read from the ROM, and is displayed in the block on the screen wherever the cursor happens to be.

Later, the color graphics adapter (CGA) was developed. It could display graphics and text, but at a much reduced resolution of 640 by 200. At about the same time, the Hercules Company developed the monographics adapter (MGA) that could display monochrome graphics and text in very high resolution. It became a de facto standard.

Then, in 1984, IBM introduced their EGA, which displayed graphics and text in 640 by 350 resolution. The adapter was priced at $995 and a high-resolution Enhanced Color Display, or monitor, was priced at $895. The clone makers immediately began turning out adapters and monitors for less than half that price. Figure 7-2 shows a Thompson enhanced graphics monitor.

Most EGA monitors can also run in MDA, CGA or EGA modes. The multisync monitors are also versatile and can be driven by almost any adapter board.

IBM's new PS/2 computers have added a fourth standard—a built-in adapter they call a VGA, or Video Graphics Adapter. These adapters have an analog output instead of the standard digital output. At the present time, only the high-resolution multisync and multiscan monitors such as NEC, Thomson, Zenith, Sony, and Taxan can be connected to the PS/2 systems.

Fig. 7-2. A high-resolution monitor. (Photo courtesy Thomson Company).

A cable adapter is all that is needed to make this setup operational. The PS/2 uses a 15-pin connector. Up until now the industry standard has been a 9 pin connector for digital monitors.

Most of the adapters set up the monitors so they display 80 characters across the screen on a single line and 25 lines from top to bottom. That means the maximum number of characters or spaces that can be typed and displayed on a screen is $80 \times 25 = 2000$. The computer considers each one of those 2000 spaces to be a block, and the screen is laid out in a grid like a sheet of graph paper. Each one of those blocks has an address. The address of the block in the upper left corner is row 0, column 0; the address of the lower right block is row 24, column 79. Software programs can send the cursor to any block on the screen.

Characters are formed within each of those 2000 blocks by the electron beam striking the phosphor pixels within that block. The medium-resolution monitors have 320 pixels, or dots, across the face of the screen and 200 pixels from the top to the bottom. This gives a total of 64,000 pixels for the entire screen. The high-resolution monitors have 640 pixels across and 200 down, for a total of 128,000. Enhanced Graphics adapters (EGA) allow 640 by 350 pixels, for a total of 224,000. Monochrome monitors can have a resolution of 720 by 350, for a total of 252,000 pixels. The new PS/2 resolution is 640 by 480, for a total of 307,200 pixels. There are several digital high-resolution monitors on the market that have even greater resolution.

A dot matrix system is used to form the characters or images. To find the number of pixels in an individual block, divide the total number of pixels listed above by 2000 blocks. For example, a 640-by-200 resolution monitor has 64 pixels per block. Because 640 pixels are used across 80 columns, these 64 pixels are arranged in an eight-by-eight matrix. A certain amount of space must be left around each character; the character created within an eight-by-eight block is formed from a matrix five pixels wide and seven pixels high. A high-resolution monochrome monitor with 720 by 350 pixels would have a 9-by-14 block. The dot-matrix character created within one of these blocks is seven pixels wide and nine pixels high.

SUPERHIGH RESOLUTION AND EGA

It won't do you any good to buy a high-resolution color monitor unless you have a high-resolution adapter that can drive it. In some cases, the adapter will cost almost as much as the monitor. the new IBM PS/2 16-inch monitor (or "color display") is $1550, but you must have an adapter for it. This adapter must use the PS/2 Micro Channel standard, and costs $1290, for a total of $2840.

At the present time, there are several high-resolution digital systems that are as good as or better than the PS/2 analog systems, and are less expensive. As I mentioned earlier, there are several systems on the market that can display either digital or analog signals. You can be sure that there will soon be many more.

When I attended the Fall 1985 COMDEX, I saw no more than a half-dozen large-screen monitors. At the 1986 show, there were hundreds of them. This is great, because competition forces innovation and lowers prices.

WHAT YOU SHOULD BUY

The determining factors in choosing a monitor should be its intended use and the amount of money you want to spend. If you can afford it, buy a large-screen, superhigh-resolution color monitor and adapter.

If you expect to do any kind of graphics, such as CAD/CAM design work, you will need a good large-screen color monitor, with very high resolution. A large screen is almost essential for some types of design drawings.

For desktop publishing, some very high-resolution monochrome monitors have been developed. Many of these monitors are designed with the long axis vertical, so that they can represent an 8½-by-11-inch sheet of paper. Instead of 25 lines, they have 66 lines, which is standard for an 11-inch sheet of paper. They also have a phosphor that will let you have black text on a white background.

For accounting, spread sheets, or word processing, a monochrome monitor is probably sufficient. I use my computer primarily for word processing, so I could get by with a monochrome monitor. Color is a bit more expensive, but I like it. After all, you only live once. To the extent that I can afford it, I want to enjoy it to the fullest. So I splurged and bought an NEC Multisync with a Vutek EGA driver.

My Vutek adapter gives me a resolution of 640 by 350. Vutek has recently developed a small plug-in board-upgrade kit, with a higher frequency crystal and software. The kit plugs into the feature connector on my Vutek board. This same feature connector is found on a large number of EGA boards. The Vutek upgrade can be used on most of these boards. With the upgrade kit, a resolution of 640 by 480 is possible on multiscan monitors. You should have a copy of Windows to take full advantage of this upgrade.

If you want to contact Vutek, their address is:

Vutek Systems
10885 Sorrento Valley Rd.
San Diego, CA 92121
(619) 587-2800

SELECTING A MONITOR

If at all possible, go to a computer show and look at the various monitors available. At a large show, you can usually find several vendors who are demonstrating their monitors, sometimes side by side. Go to several stores and compare monitors. Turn the brightness up and check the center and outer edges of the screen. Is the intensity the same in the center as at the outer edges? Check the focus, brightness, and contrast with text and graphics. There can be vast differences even in the same models from the same manufacturer. I have seen monitors that displayed the demo graphics programs beautifully, but they weren't worth a damn when displaying text in various colors.

Ask the vendor for a copy of the specifications. Check the dot pitch; for good high-resolution it should be .31 mm or less. Look for the highest horizontal and vertical frequencies. For very high resolution, the horizontal should scan at 35 to 45 kHz. The Thomson Ultrascan Model 4375 has a horizontal frequency of 15.6 kHz to 35 kHz. The vertical scan rate is 45 kHz to 75 kHz. Some of the other multisync and multiscan models respond to frequencies even broader than these.

You might also check for knobs to control and adjust the brightness, contrast, and vertical/horizontal lines. Some manufacturers place the knobs on the back or some other remote area. It is much better if they are accessible from the front so you can see what effect they have as you turn them.

I have seen some EGA monitors from the Far East selling for $350—Some of the clone EGA boards are selling for well under $200. The prices of the multisync and multiscan monitors are fairly stable because there is not much competition at the moment. The NEC Multisync, Thomson Ultrascan and others list for about $900, but many discount houses are selling them for about $550 each. These monitors can be driven by almost any EGA card, but at the present time, only the better brand-name EGAs drive the monitors to their fullest capabilities. The better adapters cost from $450 to $600 at the discount houses.

SWIVEL BASE

It might not seem important, but if at all possible, get a monitor with a swivel and tilt base. Reflections off the screen can be very disturbing. If the monitor can be tilted, you can usually eliminate this problem. You should be able to adjust it to where it is most comfortable for you to view. If several other people use the computer, chances are that they will not all be the same size, so it is nice to be able to adjust the screen for each individual. There are tilt and swivel stands that can be purchased for those monitors that do not come with one.

You will be looking at your monitor almost all of the time that you spend working with your computer. I suggest that you spend as much as you can afford to get one of the better ones.

8

Keyboards and
Other Input Devices

I am not a very good typist, but I do a lot of writing. My main reason for buying a computer several years ago was my desire to throw my old typewriter away and begin using word processing.

Typewriter keyboards are well standardized. On the other hand, I have had several computers over the last few years, and every one of them had a different keyboard. The main typewriter characters aren't changed or moved, but some of the very important control keys like ESC, CTRL, PRTSC, \, the function keys, and several others are moved all over the keyboard.

Very few of the early CP/M machines had identical keyboards, but IBM established a layout that everyone thought would be standard. See Fig. 8-1. It was an excellent keyboard—built like a Sherman tank with a very good feel. There were some minor gripes because it did not indicate CAPS or NUM LOCK mode. It also had a small RETURN key. The clone makers soon improved on this design by adding LEDs, to indicate when the CAPS and NUM locks were on, and a larger RETURN key.

About a year later, IBM came out with a keyboard that also had LED indicators and a large RETURN or ENTER key, but for some reason, they rearranged several very important keys. See Fig. 8-2. Notice that ESC, \, PRTSC, and several others were moved. These are very important keys and are used constantly. I have not been able to discover any reason as

Fig. 8-1. The original IBM keyboard layout.

to why they were moved. Because there was nothing else I could do, I accepted the new layout and have gotten used to it after a year of use. Just when I thought the new keyboard in Fig. 8-2 would be the standard, IBM released their new PS/2 line with a new keyboard layout. See Fig. 8-3.

The keyboard in Fig. 8-2 has 84 keys. The new keyboard in Fig. 8-3 has 17 more keys for a total of 101. Except for F11, F12 and PAUSE, the

Fig. 8-2. The second version.

Fig. 8-3. The latest IBM version.

other 14 additional keys are duplicates of keys that were already on the keyboard. IBM separated the numeric keypad from the alphabet keys with the four up, down, right, and left arrow keys that perform the same function as the arrows on the numeric keypad. They also installed six separate keys above the arrow keys: INSERT, HOME, PAGE UP, DELETE, END, and PAGE DOWN. These keys also perform the same function as those on the numeric key pad. They also added an extra ENTER on the numeric key pad, and there are now CTRL and ALT keys at both ends of the space bar.

The new keyboard is about one inch longer and about one inch wider than the old model, but it looks enormous when attached to the new Models 30 and 50. The old keyboard was about the same length as the PC-XT, but this keyboard has been extended to 19.4 inches long and 8.3 inches wide. The Model 30 is 16 inches wide, but the Model 50 is only 14.2 inches wide. The new keyboard is 5.2 inches longer than the Model 50 is wide.

IBM was very concerned about making a smaller footprint for the new PS/2 computers so they would not take up so much desk space, but they added over 19 square inches to the size of the keyboard.

Many people have bought programs like Framework that uses the function keys intensively. Anyone who buys a copy of Framework gets a plastic overlay for the Function keys. Many other companies offer plastic overlays that fit over the keyboard. These overlays are great for learning; even a novice can become productive in a short time. These overlays will not fit on the new keyboards.

When I sit down to write an article or a letter, time spent is not that critical. I can afford to stop and look for the right key. However, there are large businesses where the operators don't have this luxury. In many of these offices, there are hardware devices (or software programs) that count each keystroke that the operator makes during the eight-hour shift. If the operator's number of keystrokes falls below a certain level, he can be fired. This might seem harsh, but these large companies must input billions of bits of data into the computer daily.

This constant strain to maintain the keystroke quota can be as bad as the stress suffered by air traffic controllers. Can you imagine the problems these computer operators have if they must learn a new keyboard layout every so often? Change is bound to slow down productivity and must cost those large businesses millions of dollars.

Reportedly, IBM will not even offer the older keyboards as an option if you buy one of their new PS/2 machines. I'd bet next month's rent that clone keyboards will be available with the old layout.

The AT and the PS/2 keyboards have the same connectors and will plug into a PC or XT, but they will not operate interchangeably because they use different electronics and scan frequencies. Most of the clone makers install a small switch beneath their keyboards that allows them to be switched, so they can be used on a PC, XT, 80286 AT, or 80386-based machine.

SCANNERS AND OPTICAL CHARACTER READERS

If we ever run out of paper, this entire nation will suffer a crisis that will make the oil shortage seem like a very minor problem. Our nation thrives on paper. We must have three or four copies of every transaction or contract that is made. Some large corporations have multiple forms with nine or ten carbon copies. In every large office, files bulge and stacks of documents must be saved.

The advent of computers with large storage capacity was supposed to usher in a "paperless society." A vice-president of a large corporation is reported to have said that we will have a paperless society at the same time we will have paperless bathrooms.

If you have ever worked in a large company, especially one that deals with the military, you can appreciate the above statement. I worked for Lockheed Missiles and Space Company for several years. Every rivet, nut, bolt, electronic component, and anything else used in a missile is tested, tested, and retested. The results of these tests are recorded on paper, in computers on hard disks, on tape, on film, on X-rays, and in many other media. In addition, there must be three or four paper copies of nearly every one of those tests.

The Trident II missile stands 44 feet high. The employees often joked that when the height of the paperwork exceeded the height of the missile, it was almost ready to ship. A large part of the cost of military equipment is due to paperwork.

Most large companies also have mountains of memos, manuals, documents, and files that must be maintained, revised, and updated periodically. If a manual or document is in loose-leaf form, then only those pages that have changed will need to be retyped. Yet, quite often a whole manual or document will be retyped and re-issued.

Several companies now manufacture optical character readers (OCR) that can scan a line of printed type, recognize each character, and put that character in a computer as if it were typed in from a keyboard. Once the data is in the computer, a word processor can be used to revise the data and then print them out again.

The data could also be entered into a computer and stored on floppies, a hard disk, or on CD-ROM so that it takes less space to store.

Data in a computer can be searched very quickly. I have spent hours going through printed manuals looking for certain items. If the data had been in a computer, I could have found the information in minutes.

Optical character readers have been around for several years. When they first came out, they cost from $6,000 to more than $15,000. They were very limited in the character fonts (type styles) they could recognize and were not able to handle graphics at all.

However, vast improvements have been made in the last few years. Many OCRs are now fairly inexpensive, starting at about $900. There are also some very sophisticated commercial models, such as the Palantir and Kurzweil, that cost as much as $40,000. Many of the more expensive ones have the ability to recognize a large number of fonts and graphics. Of course, there are more bells and whistles as you move from the $900 models up to the $40,000 ones.

The Houston Instruments Company specializes in manufacturing plotters. They have developed a scanning head for one of their plotters that can scan a large drawing, digitize the lines and symbols, and then put them in a computer. The drawing can then be changed and replotted very easily.

Scanners are essential if you plan to do any serious desktop publishing. I will list the names and addresses of some of the scanner companies in Chapter 11.

MICE

I have never used a Macintosh, but they look like toys to me. I never understood why so many were sold. Then, I talked to a friend who is an editor. She knows very little about DOS and really doesn't have the time to learn. With a Macintosh, she doesn't have to know much about computers. With the pull-down menus and the mouse, all she has to do is point and click.

I have seen her take prose that I had written, rewritten, pored over, polished, and perfected, and with her mouse and Macintosh, she chopped, deleted and rearranged it so that it was completely unrecognizable in just seconds.

The Macintosh is easy to use. The MS-DOS world has finally realized this and we now have several good software programs with Macintosh-like menus. There are also dozens of companies who are manufacturing mice (or is it mouses?) and there are no standards. Each company makes its own software driver which is usually supplied on a disk.

Some use optics with an LED that shines on a reflective grid. As the mouse is moved across the grid, the reflected light is picked up by a detector and sent to the computer to move the cursor. For work that demands very close tolerances, the spacing of the grid lines might not provide sufficient resolution. You might be better off with a mouse that utilizes a ball. Ball-type mice afford smooth and continuous movement of the cursor. You don't need a grid for the ball-type mice, but you do need about a square foot of clear desk space to move the mouse about. The ball picks up dirt, so it should be cleaned often.

Most mice require an external power source. Some come with a small plug-in transformer that should be plugged into your power strip. Most of them also require a serial port for their input to the computer. Most AT mother boards have at least one serial port built onto the board, but you will still need a cable that connects the port to the outside world. You will also need a serial port for a modem. The AT can support COM1 and COM2 for a mouse and a modem or serial printer.

The Honeywell Disc Instruments Company has developed a "trackball" cursor device that looks much like the ball on some video games. The trackball has a connector that plugs in series with your keyboard connector. This device draws electricity from the same line that feeds your keyboard. The trackball is an integral unit about four inches wide by five inches long, so it does not require as much desk space as the other types. See Fig. 8-4.

I am using an IMSI mouse. It has a ball and is similar to the Logitech mouse. The IMSI mouse has a connector that plugs in series with my keyboard connector. From this connection with my keyboard cable, it derives its 5-volt power supply. See Fig. 8-5.

There is still only limited software that allows you to use a mouse. More are being developed every day. The PS/2 system has a built-in port for a "pointing device."

IBM has blessed Windows, a program that was developed by Microsoft, the company that developed PC-DOS and MS-DOS. Microsoft is working diligently to develop OS/2. There are other Windows-like

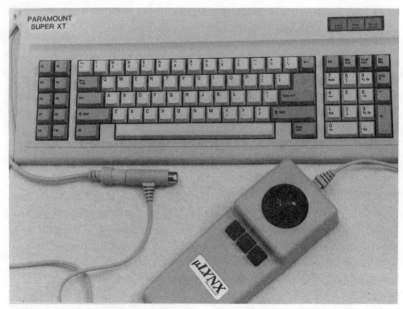

Fig. 8-4. A trackball device for cursor control.

programs, such as IBM's own TopView and Digital Research's GEM series; however, because Windows has been endorsed by IBM, it will become the standard.

Windows can be used with many programs, yet to realize this program's many benefits, it is almost essential that a mouse be used.

BAR CODES

Bar codes are a system of black and white lines that are arranged much like the Morse code of dots and dashes. Any numeral or letter of the alphabet can be represented with combinations of wide and narrow bars and wide and narrow spaces.

Bar codes were first adopted by retail grocers. They assigned a unique number, the Universal Product Code (UPC), to just about every manufactured and pre-packaged product sold in grocery stores. Different sizes of the same product have unique numbers assigned to each. The same types of products from different manufacturers also have unique numbers. Many large grocery stores now sell everything from automobile parts to drugs, and each product has its own unique bar code number.

When the clerk runs an item across the scanner, the dark bars absorb light and the white bars reflect light. The scanner decodes a number and sends it to the main computer. The computer then matches that number to the unique number stored on its hard disk which has the price of that

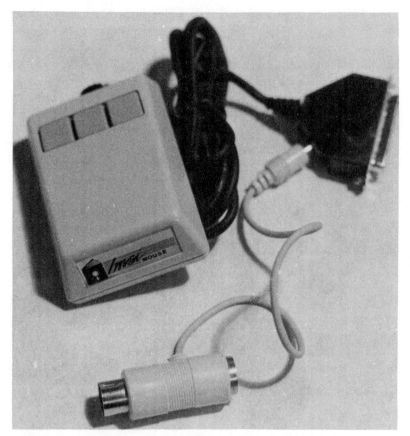

Fig. 8-5. A mouse. Note that it connects in series with the keyboard.

product, a description, the amount in inventory, and other data about the item. The computer sends back the price and description of the item to the cash register, where it is printed out. The computer then deducts that item from the inventory and adds the price to the cash received for the day.

At the end of the day, the manager can look at the computer output and know exactly how much business was done, what inventories need to be replenished, and what products were the biggest sellers. With the push of a button, he or she can change any or all of the prices in the store.

In the mid-1970s, the Department of Defense (DOD) started looking for a better way to keep track of its huge inventories. It set up a committee and, in 1982, this committee decreed that all military materiel sold to the government would have bar-code labels. Many of the suppliers screamed because this added to their costs. But these costs were really passed on to the government, so they weren't too much of a burden.

It wasn't long before many of the people who had complained about having to use the bar codes were using them in many ways to increase productivity. There are very few businesses, large or small, that cannot benefit from the use of bar codes.

There are several different types of bar-code readers or scanners. Some are actually small, portable computers that can store data and then be downloaded into a larger system. Some scanners can be interfaced with a PC, XT, or AT.

There are several companies that make Point of Sale (POS) systems, with a bar code reader, a computer, and a cash drawer all integrated into a single unit. Some of these POS systems can be tied together in a local area network.

A bar-code scanner can read data into a computer at about 1700 characters per minute with absolute accuracy. Do you know anyone who can type that fast?

If you are interested in bar-code technology, there is a free magazine to which you should subscribe. It is called *ID Systems*. Write them for a subscription qualifying form at:

ID Systems
174 Concord St.
Peterborough, NH 03458
(603) 924-9631

COMPUTER VISION

Many companies have set up cameras to control their production lines. Some inspect the items as they came off the assembly line. The image of a "golden" circuit board that is perfect in its component placement and appearance is digitized and stored in the computer. Each time a circuit board comes off the line, the camera focuses on it and the computer compares it to the stored image. If the two images match, the board is sent on to be further assembled or electronically tested. A computer can check a circuit board (or a lot of other things) much faster, more accurately, and more consistently than a human being.

COMPUTERIZED VOICE OUTPUT

Computer-synthesized voice systems have been developed to do hundreds of tasks. Sensors can be set up so that when a light beam is broken, they send a signal to a computer to, for example, alert a person of danger. The Atlanta airport has an underground shuttle to move people to the various airline gates. It has several sensors that feed into a computer.

If a person is standing in the doorway it will ask the person to move, and the train will not move until it is safe to do so.

Many automated banking systems allow you to dial a telephone line into a computer. A computerized voice asks questions and lets you pay your bills, transfer funds, and do almost all of your banking by telephone.

The telephone system has computerized voices for the time and for information. Many more uses are being developed every day.

VOICE DATA INPUT

Another way to put data into a computer is to talk to it through a microphone. Of course, you need the electronics that can take the signal created by the microphone, detect spoken words and turn them into digital information that the computer can use.

The early voice data-input systems were very expensive and limited. One reason was that voice technology required lots of memory, but the cost of memory has dropped considerably in the last few years and technology has improved in many other ways.

Voice technology involves "training" a computer to recognize a word spoken by a person. When you speak into a microphone, the sound waves cause a diaphragm or some other device to move back and forth in a magnetic field and create a current that is analogous to the sound wave. If this current is recorded and played through a good audio system, the loudspeaker will respond to the amplified signal and reproduce a sound that is similar to the one at the microphone.

A person can speak a word into a microphone that creates a unique signal for that word and that particular person's voice. The signal is fed into an electronic circuit and its pattern is digitized and stored in the computer. If several words are spoken, the circuit will digitize and store each one. Each word will have a distinct pattern. Later, when the computer hears a word, it will search through the patterns that it has stored, to see if that word matches any of its stored words.

Of course, once the computer is able to recognize a word, it can perform some useful work. You could command it to load and run a program or perform any of several other tasks.

Since every person's voice is different, the computer would not recognize the voice of anyone who had not trained it. Training the computer may involve saying the same word several times so that the computer can store several patterns of the person's voice.

Voice-data input is useful whenever you must use both hands to do a job, but you still need a computer to perform certain tasks. One area where voice data is used extensively is in new military fighter planes. They move so fast that the pilot does not have time to manipulate computer keys and he usually already has both hands full. However, he can have the computer do hundreds of jobs just by telling it what he wants done.

Voice data is also useful on production lines where the operator does not have time to enter data manually. They can also be used in a laboratory where a technician is looking through a microscope and cannot pause to write down data. There are instances where the person might have to be several feet from the computer and still be able to input data through the microphone lines. The person might even be miles away and be able to transmit data over a telephone line.

In most of the systems in use today, the computer must be trained to recognize a specific word, so the vocabulary is limited. However, every spoken word can be represented by just 42 *phonemes* (the smallest units of speech). Several companies are working on systems that will take a sample of a person's voice that contains all these phonemes. Using the phonemes from this sample, the computer could then recognize any word that the person speaks. Eventually there will be typewriters that can perfectly transcribe dictation. Robots will understand oral commands and perform thousands of tasks, giving us with more time to play with our computers.

9

Memory

Memory is one of the most crucial elements of the computer. During use, software programs are placed into random access memory (RAM). Here data is manipulated, calculations are performed, data bases are searched, and so forth.

RAM is an electronic blackboard. But unlike information on an ordinary blackboard, RAM's information must be actively maintained. If the computer is turned off or if it loses power and the data in RAM has not been saved to disk, it is gone forever.

Read Only Memory (ROM) is another kind of memory. We can read from or write to RAM, but ROM can only be read, usually only by the computer. It usually contains instructions and rules, such as those contained in the BIOS ROM that controls the operation of the computer.

REAL MEMORY

The 8088- and 8086-based machines can address one megabyte of memory. Each one of those million bytes has a unique address, much like the individual house addresses in a city. The CPU can go to any one of those addresses and read data from, or write data to, that address. It takes a minimum of 20 lines on the standard bus to address one megabyte ($2^{20} = 1,048,576$).

The memory addresses are stacked, starting with 0 at the bottom and going up to the one megabyte limit. Only the bottom 640 K is available for DOS and application programs. Just above the 640 K is 128 K that is reserved for video. The top 256 K is reserved for ROM BIOS. The 640 K that is available to the user is called *real* memory.

EXPANDED MEMORY

The 80286 CPU is capable of addressing 16 megabytes. Although the 80286 is much faster and more efficient than the 8088 or 8086, it has the same 640 K DOS-imposed memory limitation. It will be capable of directly addressing the full 16 megabyts of memory when the new OS/2 is released.

Table 9-1 shows how the memory is stacked:

There are several large programs that need much more than 640 K. A large business using Lotus 1-2-3 or a large database program might need several megabytes of memory.

In a rare instance of cooperation among corporations, Lotus, Intel, and Microsoft adopted a system for using expanded memory on PCs, XTs, and ATs. They called it the Lotus-Intel-Microsoft Expanded Memory Specification (LIM EMS).

With this system, up to eight megabytes of memory can be installed on boards and plugged into the computer's expansion slots. See Fig. 9-1. Memory on the boards is divided into pages of 16 K each. Hardware circuits on the board and software programs can switch the various pages in and out of RAM.

The AST and Quadram Corporations are leading manufacturers of plug-in boards. Ashton-Tate is the publisher of dBASE III, Framework II, and several other programs. These three corporations decided that the LIM EMS system could be improved. They cooperated to develop the AST-Quadram-Ashton-Tate Enhanced Expanded Memory Specification (AQA EEMS). This specification is a bit more versatile than LIM EMS.

EXTENDED MEMORY Up to 15 megabytes in 80286 Protected Mode.
ROM BIOS 256 K reserved space
VIDEO 128 K reserved space
RAM 640 K for DOS and applications programs

Table 9-1. Memory Arrangement.

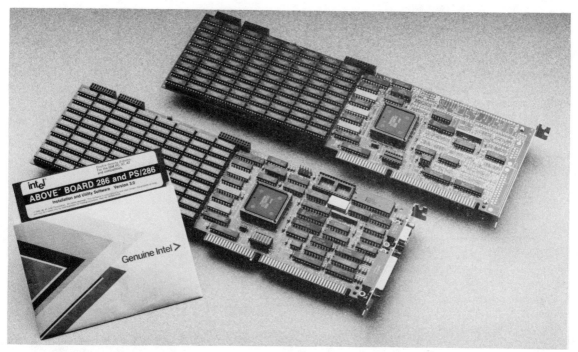

Fig. 9-1. Intel Above Boards. (Photo courtesy Intel Corp.)

There are several companies in the United States and overseas who are manufacturing boards with large amounts of memory. Many of these boards do not support the EMS or EEMS specifications. Some of them are very slow, can take hours to perform a task that an AST RAMpage or an Intel Above Board can do in minutes.

The First Amendment to the Constitution guarantees freedom of speech. It says nothing at all about truthfulness of speech. The people who write the ads for computer products (and other products) use the First Amendment to the hilt. Those who write ads for memory boards are no exception. Although memory chips are coming down in price, memory boards are still expensive, at $500 to $1800.

Some firms advertise a two-Megabyte board for a fairly low price, but if you look closely at the ad, this could be with 0 K memory. This does not mean that the memory is ''OK''. It means that there is no memory installed at the price advertised.

Since these are fairly high-cost items, it is worthwhile to have the vendor demonstrate the board with a large file. If it is a clone, or a lesser-known brand, you might have him compare it with a well-known brand, such as Intel's Above Board or AST's RAMpage. There are some clones that are very good and sell for about half the cost of major brand-names.

EMS EMULATION

There are several companies who have developed software programs that can act as expanded memory managers. The March 31 issue of *PC Magazine* reviewed five software programs, each costing less than $100, that let you use extended memory or a hard disk to swap 16 K pages of memory back and forth. Of course, at this price, you cannot expect them to be as fast or have the options offered by the high-cost, brand-name boards. Those using a hard disk can be especially slow. But if you have more time than money, it is a good solution for an occasional large memory need.

Here are the addresses of the five software companies:

LIMSIM
Larson Computing
1556 Halford Ave. #142
Santa Clara, CA 95051
(408) 737-0627

EMSimulator
Kam & Associates
3615 Harding Ave. #401
Honolulu, HI 96816
(808) 737-3647

Micro VMS
Vericomp
8825 Aero Dr. #210
San Diego, CA 92123
(619) 277-0400

Above Disc
Tele-Ware West
909 Electric Ave. #202
Seal Beach, CA 90740
(800) 654-5301

V-EMM
Fort's Software
P.O. Box 396
Manhattan, KS 66502
(913) 537-2897

ACCESSING EXTENDED MEMORY

There is a difference between expanded memory and extended memory. *Extended* memory is memory installed on an 80286 system directly above the one megabyte of standard memory. Extended memory cannot be installed on a PC or XT because the 8088 or 8086 has no provision for addressing more than one megabyte, but *expanded* memory boards can be used on a PC or XT.

Many AT mother boards are sold with one megabyte of memory installed on them, but 384 K of that is extended memory and is not directly addressable by DOS. However, if you have DOS 3.0 or later, you can make limited use of this memory by using the VDISK.SYS device driver.

You should have a CONFIG.SYS file in your root directory. It is a file that allows you to configure your computer to handle many devices and peripherals. It lends a tremendous versatility to your computer. It is stored in the root directory and is run each time the computer is booted up. To look at it, go to your root directory and type TYPE CONFIG.SYS. This is what my CONFIG.SYS file looks like:

```
DEVICE = DMDRVR.BIN
BUFFERS = 40
FILES = 30
DEVICE = ANSI.SYS
DEVICE = VDISK,SYS 384/E
```

The first device in my CONFIG.SYS file is the disk manager driver from ONTRACK Computer Systems. This driver allows me to bypass the DOS 32-megabyte hard disk limit and use my 60-megabyte hard disk.

The computer stores data in RAM buffers as they are read from and written to disk. It is similar to a cache system. The number of buffers can be almost any size you want. If your programs do a lot of reading and writing to disk, it is best to have 30 or 40 buffers.

The FILES number is the number of files that can be open at one time. It may not be necessary, depending on the type of computing you do.

The ANSI.SYS is a driver provided by DOS that enables you to control the video screen's color and graphics. It also allows you to reprogram the keyboard.

The VDISK.SYS is another driver that is provided by DOS 3.0 and later versions to allow the use of a virtual disk. The VDISK.SYS allows you to create an imaginary floppy disk from the extended memory. The ＼E is necessary because I have two floppies, A: and B: and my hard disk is partitioned into C: and D:, so the RAM disk becomes drive E:.

The RAM E: drive can be used just like any other drive. You can copy files into it, or from it, or use it as a very fast floppy. However, you must remember that it is volatile memory and all data will disappear if it is not saved to disk before the computer is turned off.

If you want to change your CONFIG.SYS file, you can do so by typing COPY CON CONFIG.SYS. Press ENTER, then type the number of buffers, files, and devices that you want in your file. Press ENTER or RETURN after each line. When you are finished, press F6 to end the file. When you press F6 or CONTROL Z, DOS will tell you that one file has been copied. The CONFIG.SYS file is only run when the computer is booted up so anything you change will not be in effect until you reboot the computer.

You can also use the DOS EDLIN command to edit the CONFIG.SYS file, or it can be copied into a word processor, like WordStar, edited, and copied back to the root directory.

PROTECTED MODE

The 80286 has the capability of working in two different modes, the *real* mode and the *protected* mode. In the real mode, the 80286 processes data much the same way an 8088 or 8086 does, but it does it faster and more efficiently. In the protected mode it will run several programs at the same time, or *multitask*. In this mode barriers will be erected to *protect* any program that is running from interfering with any other one.

The protected mode allows the 80286 to address extended memory of up to 16 megabytes. The protected mode will also allow the computer to have a virtual memory of as much as one gigabyte. Remember, virtual means that it appears to be present. A very large hard disk could be used as virtual memory by an 80286.

This amazing chip has all these capabilities and more, but none of them can be utilized until the new OS/2 operating system is released.

THE NEW OS/2 SYSTEM

When the new operating system (OS/2) is released, we still will not be able to utilize all the capabilities of the 80286 because the necessary software has yet to be written. Most of this software can only be written after the programmers have had a chance to explore the OS/2 system.

OS/2 is supposed to be released in early 1988, but developing it is not a simple task, and some think that it might be delayed. The price for the initial release has already been set at $325. This is a bit high, but if it does all that it is supposed to do, it will make a lot of people happy.

THE ADVANTAGES OF A BABY AT MOTHER BOARD

Many people have spent $1000 or more on accelerator boards or boards with 80286 processors to plug into a PC or XT. These accelerator boards will not allow the PC or XT to take advantage of OS/2's full capabilities. Instead, you should pull out the 8088 mother board and install a Baby AT board. This can be done for $300 to $700.

This is a relatively inexpensive way to upgrade an older machine and vastly increase its power and capabilities. If you use a PC or XT for any serious computing at all, then I would recommend this course of action. It is really not that difficult and is well worth the effort and expense.

10
Printers

You will need a printer to go with your computer. Depending on what you are going to use your computer for, you might need two or more. You should consider several factors when you decide to buy one. The first consideration, of course, is what use you plan for your printer. Will you be doing any graphics or desktop publishing? Will you need a wide carriage, a tractor feed, or multiple paper feed bins? Will your printer be connected to more than one computer? What size buffer do you need? Do you want IBM graphics compatibility? Most importantly, how much money do you want to spend?

TYPES OF PRINTERS

There are two main types of printers: dot matrix and letter quality. The dot matrix is usually faster than letter quality. The dot-matrix print head has a single, vertical row of pins. Some less expensive printers have only 9 pins, and the more expensive printers might have 18 to 24. As the head moves in discrete increments across the paper, electronic solenoids push individual pins forward to form characters. *Note: The solenoids in a print head generate a powerful magnetic field. Do not place your floppy disks near them while they are printing.*

Here is a representation of the pins in a nine-pin dot-matrix print head and how it would form the letter A:

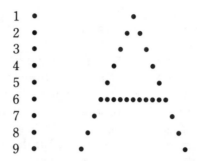

The print head moves from left to right. The numbers on the left represent the individual pins in the head. The first pin to be struck would be number 9, then number 8, then 7, 6, 5, 6 and 4, 3, 6 and 2, 1, 6 and 2, 3, 6 and 4, 5, 6, 7, 8, and 9. This single pass would give a fast draft-quality character. It would be fast, but the dots would be large and distinct enough to be noticeable. If it was to be near-letter-quality, each pin would be stuck, then the head would move slightly, and each pin would be struck again. Shifting the head and striking the pins a second time fills in the spaces between the dots and causes the character to be more solid.

This method gives near-letter-quality printing (NLQ), but striking each pin twice reduces the print speed by about half. If the printer has 18 or 24 pins in the head, the pins are smaller and closer together. They can print a fairly decent character in one fast draft mode pass, but draft print is usually fairly light, so for NLQ most of the 18- and 24-pin printers still must offset the head and strike each pin twice. The quality of the print from 18- and 24-pin printers can be very close to that of daisy wheel printers.

Speed, measured in characters per second (CPS) is a factor to be considered when choosing a printer. You want one that is as fast as possible. Waiting for a long document to print out can be frustrating. Depending on the type of printer and computer you have, your system will probably be tied up for as long as it takes to print out the document. This could get expensive in a business office if the employee has to wait until the printing is finished, so a high-speed printer is desirable in most cases.

Draft quality is often sufficient for such things as informal notes, memos, and preliminary reports. A quick draft copy is easier to edit and proofread than text on a screen. Most monitors display only 25 lines, and many word processors use 10 to 15 of those lines for menus and help, which means you can only see a portion of the page at any one time. It's best to print out a rough draft and do your proofing on hard copy. When you have made all the necessary changes and polished it into a real gem, then use the slower NLQ mode.

Many better dot-matrix printers can print several different font styles and sizes. There are several software programs that can be used to print out signs, banners, and all sorts of graphics.

Some manufacturers advertise draft speeds as high as 400 CPS in draft mode, but few claim more than 100 CPS in NLQ mode. Speed tests performed by *Byte Magazine* and others show that most vendors exaggerate their CPS claims. There is no standard speed test, and it takes less time to print certain characters than others, so a printer might achieve 400 CPS in a burst of speed during the middle of a line, but the time required to print every character of the alphabet and execute carriage returns and line feeds would reduce the figure somewhat.

There are absolutely no standards for printers. Every manufacturer dreams up his own character fonts and drivers. Software publishers must supply hundreds of different drivers with their software packages to make them compatible with a wide variety of printers. The closest thing to a standard is the character and graphics set first used by Epson. IBM bought the small Epson dot-matrix printers and put their logo on them. This helped establish something resembling a standard. Most of the printer makers are still installing their own drivers, but many of them are including emulation firmware for the IBM and Epson standard.

The cost of dot-matrix printers can range from $200 to over $2000, depending on the speed, special features, and other extras.

EXTRAS

Printer selection also involves a consideration of the following features:

Wide Carriage

Most printers come in at least two different widths. I prefer the wide carriage. Quite often I want to address a large manila envelope, which requires a wide carriage. If you are in a business office, there might be times when you will need to do graphics or need the wide paper for a spreadsheet printout.

The wide carriage models may cost $100 to $200 more than the standard size. Otherwise, they usually have the same speed and letter quality specifications.

Tractors

Tractors are the sprockets that engage the holes in the margins of continuous-feed paper. Most printers have standard friction feed for printing individually cut sheets. Several printers have built-in tractors, but some offer the tractor only as an added-cost option that can cost $75 to $100 extra. Tractors are essential when making labels or other types of work where the paper must be controlled. Most friction feeds will not hold the paper straight or provide accurate and consistent line feed, especially after the platen gets old and hardened. Therefore I recommend that you get a printer with a tractor.

Paper Advance

Most printers have a couple of buttons that advance the paper. One might be marked "top of form" and the other marked "paper feed." The TOP OF FORM button moves a sheet of paper forward to the top of the next sheet. The paper feed button advances the paper one line at a time for as long as the button is held down.

Most printers also have a large knob attached to the platen, which can be turned to position the paper. You should not use this knob when the power is on, because it works against the electric clutches that advance the paper. This could damage and wear out the clutches. If you want to use the knob to position the paper, switch off the power first.

Buffers

Even a very high-speed printer is slow compared to how fast a computer can feed data to it. If the printer has a large buffer, the computer can dump its data into the buffer and be free for other work. If the printer is in a large office, a large stand-alone buffer might be worth the cost.

Print Spoolers

Print spoolers are similar to buffers, but they use a portion of your computer's RAM memory to store the print data. Some programs store the data on your hard disk and spool it out to the printer as needed. The computer will then be free. SPOOL is an acronym for Simultaneous Peripheral Operation On Line.

Several multifunction boards, such as the AST and Paradise boards, come with print spooler software programs. Public-domain spooler programs are on many bulletin boards. Such programs are also available from companies, such as PC-SIG Library and MicroCom Systems, that supply public domain software. (For addresses see Chapter 14.)

Multiple Bins

Some printers will allow you to attach several different paper bins to them. Standard-size cut-sheet paper could be in one bin, the long legal-size in another, and envelopes in a third bin. Some bins are expensive, especially those designed for laser printers.

Colors

Some printers can use a wide ribbon that has three or more colors on it. The printer can shift the ribbon to the desired color and blend the colors. Hewlett-Packard has announced an ink-jet printer that can print seven-color graphics.

Sound Proofing

Printers can be very noisy. In a large office, they can be disruptive. Several companies manufacture sound-proof enclosures. These are usually made from plywood and lined with foam rubber. They usually have a clear plastic door so you can see what is going on inside. These enclosures can be expensive and cost from $150 to over $200. If you don't have that kind of money, you might take a large cardboard box and put it over the printer. You can also eliminate a lot of printer noise simply by placing foam rubber beneath the printer.

Stands

There are several stands that raise the printer off the table so that a stack of fanfold computer paper can be placed beneath the printer. They cost from $20 to $75. I have my printer sitting on a couple bricks, and I put foam rubber on top of the bricks to eliminate some of the noise.

Fonts

Many printers now have little doors that will accept cartridges for several different fonts. If you do any fancy printing, these fonts can be valuable.

LETTER QUALITY

Daisy-wheel printers give excellent letter-quality type. Most letter-quality printers use a daisy wheel, a thimble, or some other device that has characters formed on it. Compared to dot-matrix printers, they are very slow. They usually print at 10 to 45 CPS. As the daisy wheel spins, a solenoid pushes a pin or hammer forward to strike the individual characters, pushing them against the ribbon and paper. The daisy wheel continues to spin as the characters are being struck. It takes precise timing for the hammer to hit a character and release it while the wheel is spinning.

Different fonts are available for daisy-wheel printers. Most daisy wheels are very easy to replace, so you can easily change the print style.

Many of the newer dot-matrix machines have print quality that is almost as good as the daisy wheel. They are also much faster and have many capabilities that the daisy wheel does not, such as a higher draft speed and a wider variety of fonts, changeable by software during the printout.

Sales of daisy-wheel printers are declining. The cost of daisy wheel printers ranges from $400 to $3000, depending on speed, buffer sizes, and other features.

The daisy wheel is not yet dead. There are some instances in business where the printout must be letter perfect. A letter from the president of a large firm, asking a bank for a loan of a million dollars, might not get much attention if it is printed at draft speed on a nine-pin, dot-matrix printer.

After several years of faithful service, I retired my old Brother HR1 daisy wheel and bought a Star NB24-15. Although it can't print with quite the same quality, it can print a page about 10 times faster than my old Brother and I am quite happy with it.

RIBBONS

Most dot-matrix printers use nylon cloth ribbons. They are relatively inexpensive and durable. Most ribbons cost between four and ten dollars each. Kits are available that can be used to re-ink the ribbons. After the kit is paid for, it costs only pennies to re-ink a ribbon. The ribbons can be used until the fabric wears out.

Many letter-quality printers use carbon-film ribbons. They give good, crisp letters. Cloth ribbons may also be used, but they cannot produce the same quality print. Carbon-film ribbons are good for a single pass only; there is no way that they can be re-inked or used again. Some printers use a wide ribbon in a cartridge. The ribbon carriage moves the ribbon up and down so that three characters can be struck across the width of the ribbon. One of these ribbons will allow several thousand characters to be printed in a single pass.

Both cloth and carbon-film ribbons are available in various colors. Most ribbons are on cartridges, so it is fairly easy to stop the printer and change colors. A little color is a great way to grab attention or to emphasize a point.

LASER PRINTERS

Laser printers have been around several years. Some of the early ones cost as much as $100,000. There are still some very sophisticated ones that cost that much and more. Laser printers combine laser and reproduction technologies. A laser writes the characters on a large rotating drum similar to the one used in copying machines. This drum then prints a whole sheet of paper in one rotation.

Canon is a Japanese company that makes dozens of major electronic products. They are one of the leading manufacturers of reproduction machines. About five years ago, they developed a laser printer that cost about $10,000. A short time later Hewlett-Packard, using the Canon "engine," developed their Laserjet, which cost about $3600. The HP Laserjet has become the de facto standard for laser printers.

During the last few years, dozens of companies have developed laser printers. Most of them use the same type of engine used in the HP Laserjet.

Recently Ricoh, another large Japanese company, developed a slightly different laser engine. See Fig. 10-1. It is about one-third smaller than the Canon-type engines. This has encouraged more companies to enter the laser business using the Ricoh engine.

This competition has been a great benefit to consumers. It has forced many improvements, and the discount price for some models is now down to $1500. I have no doubt that prices will drop even more as the competition increases and the economies of scale in manufacturing becomes greater.

EXTRAS

Don't be surprised if you go into a store to buy a $1500 machine and end up paying twice that much. The $1500 advertised price may be for a bare bones model without several of the essential items needed to do any productive work. Plug-in font cartridges, memory, controller boards, and software might all cost extra. Some paper feeders may cost as much as the basic printer.

Memory

If you plan to do any graphics or desktop publishing (DTP), you will

Fig. 10-1. A laser printer. (Photo courtesy Ricoh Corp.)

need to have at least one megabyte of memory in the machine. Of course, the more memory, the better. It will cost about $500 extra for 1.5 megabytes of memory and about $2000 for an extra 4.5 megabytes.

Page Description Languages

If you plan to do any desktop publishing, you might also need a page-description language (PDL) controller board. As I pointed out in the chapter on monitors, text characters and graphics images are two different species. Monitor controller boards usually have all of the alphanumeric characters stored in ROM. When you press the letter A on the keyboard, the ROM chip is referenced and the A is produced and displayed in the screen block where the cursor happens to be. Another set of chips stores the symbols used to create graphics displays. Some of the early monitor drivers were capable of producing text only.

Laser printers are similar to monitors and drivers. They need a special controller to mix and print images or graphics and text on the same page. Several companies have developed their own PDLs. None of them are compatible with each other. This is a major problem for software developers, because they must try to include drivers for each PDL.

The Apple LaserWriter used Adobe System's PostScript PDL. IBM has recently announced that they will also be using it. Soon after, Hewlett-Packard said it would adopt it, so PostScript is almost certain to become the standard page-description language.

Speed

Laser printers can print from six to ten pages per minute. However, some complex graphics may require more than one minute to print a single page.

Color

Several companies are working to develop a color laser printer. There are some big problems to overcome. If and when color is available, the cost will probably be from $15,000 to $25,000.

Resolution

Almost all laser printers have 300-by-300 dots per inch resolution, which is very good, but not nearly as good as the 1200-by-1200 dots per inch typeset used in standard publishing.

Maintenance

Most laser printers use a toner cartridge that is good for 3000 to 5000 pages. The original cost of the cartridge is about $100. Several small companies are now refilling the spent cartridges for about $50 each.

There are other maintenance costs. Since these machines are very similar to the copying machines, they have moving parts that can wear out and jam. Most of the larger companies give a mean time between failures (MTBF) of 30,000 to 100,000 pages. Remember that these are only average figures and not a guarantee.

LIGHT-EMITTING DIODE PRINTERS

Light-emitting diode (LED) systems have also been developed, using technology similar to the laser system. Instead of using a laser beam to write images on the rotating drum, a row of densely-packed LEDs, as many as 400 per inch, are turned on and off to expose the photo-receptor drum. Manufacturers claim that the LED printers are more reliable and require less maintenance than the lasers.

OTHER TYPES OF PRINTERS

Several other types of printers are available. Thermal printers are relatively inexpensive. They use heat to darken specially treated paper. They are quieter than the impact-type printers, but the print quality can be rather poor.

Ink-jet printers spray ink onto the paper to form characters. They are quiet because there is no impact. Hewlett-Packard is the major manufacturer of these printers. They are also small and capable of printing in various colors.

PLOTTERS

Plotters are devices that can draw almost any shape. A plotter can have up to seven different colored pens. The pens are quite similar to ball point pens. The plotter arm can be directed to choose any of the pens. This arm is attached to a sliding rail and can be moved from one side of the paper to the other. A solenoid can lower the pen at any spot on the paper to write. While one motor is moving the arm horizontally, a second motor moves the paper vertically beneath the arm. This motor can move the paper to any spot, and the pen can be lowered to write on that spot. The motors are controlled by X-Y coordinates. They can move the pen and paper in very small increments, so almost any design can be traced out.

Plotters are ideal for printing out circuit board designs, architectural drawings, transparencies for overhead projection, graphs, charts, and many CAD/CAM drawings. All of these can be done in as many as seven different colors.

There are several different plotter sizes. Some desktop units are limited to only A- and B-size plots. There are large floor-standing models that can accept paper four feet wide and several feet long.

A desk model costs from $200 to $2000. A large floor-standing model costs from $4000 to $10,000. If you are doing very precise work, such as designing a transparency that will be photographed and used to make a circuit board, you will want one of the more accurate and expensive machines.

There are many very good graphics programs available that can use plotters, and there are several manufacturers of plotters, but there are no standards. As with the printers, each company has developed its own drivers. This is very frustrating for software developers, who must try to include in their programs drivers for all brands of hardware. If you buy a software program that cannot drive your particular plotter, you will be SOL (Sorry, Out of Luck).

Hewlett-Packard has been one of the major plotter manufacturers. Many of the other manufacturers now emulate the HP drivers. Almost all of the software that requires a plotter includes a driver for HP. If you are in the market for a plotter, make sure it can emulate the HP.

Houston Instruments is also a major manufacturer of plotters. Their plotters are somewhat less expensive than Hewlett-Packard's.

One of the disadvantages of plotters is that they are slow. There are now some software programs that will allow a laser printer to act as a plotter. Of course, a laser printer is limited to 8½-by-11-inch sheets of paper.

PORTS

The computer allows four ports: two serial and two parallel. A plotter, dot matrix, daisy wheel, or laser printer will require one of these ports. If you have a serial printer, you will need a board with an RS-232C connector. The parallel printers use Centronics-type connectors. When you buy your printer, buy a cable that is configured for your printer and your computer.

Most standard AT-size mother boards have a parallel and serial port built-in, but these ports are often only a couple rows of pins soldered to the mother board. To use them, you will need a cable with connectors that will plug into these pins. These mother boards usually have a switch or shorting bar that enables or disables the on-board ports.

INTERFACES

Printers can be very difficult to interface. In the serial system, bits are transmitted one bit at a time. The parallel system uses an eight-line bus and eight bits are transmitted at a time, one bit on each line. It takes eight bits to make one character, so with the parallel system, a whole character can be transmitted on the eight lines at one time.

The parallel system was developed by the Centronics Company. IBM adopted the parallel system as the default mode for their PC and PC-XT. The clones followed suit, so parallel inputs are standard on most printers sold today. Many printers will accept either parallel or serial data.

You can buy printer boards with parallel or serial outputs. Some multifunction boards provide both.

PRINTER SHARING

Ordinarily, a printer will sit idle most of the time. There are some days when I don't even turn my printer on. There are usually several computers in most large offices and businesses. Arrangements can be made so that a printer or plotter can be used by several computers.

If there are only two or three computers and they are fairly close together, such arrangements are easy. There are manual switch boxes that cost from $45 to $150 which allow any one of two or three computers to be switched on-line to a printer. With a simple switch box, if the computers use the standard parallel ports, the cables from the computers to the printer should be no more than ten feet long. Parallel signals begin to degrade if the cable is longer than ten feet and data can be lost.

If the computers are more than ten feet from the printer, then the serial ports should be used. A serial cable can be longer than 30 feet without any problems. This requires a printer that is capable of accepting a serial input.

If the printer has only a parallel input, it is possible to buy a serial-to-parallel converter. A fairly long serial cable can be used, then the signals can be converted to parallel just before the cable is connected to the printer.

If the serial port of a computer is used, you must use the DOS MODE command to switch from parallel output to serial. For years I used a serial daisy-wheel printer. The following command was part of my AUTOEXEC.BAT and was loaded into memory every time I booted up my computer:

```
MODE COM1:1200,N,8,P.
MODE LPT1:=COM1.
```

This says that the device hooked to the COM1 port uses 1200 baud with no parity, has 8 bits, and is a printer. The baud rate for printers ranges from 300 to 9600, so it should be set accordingly. The second line says that LPT1, which is the number one parallel port, has been switched to COM1, which is the number one serial port.

Several electronic switching devices are available. Some are very sophisticated and can allow a large number of different types of computers to be attached to a single printer or plotter. Many of them have built-in buffers and allow cable lengths of more than 250 feet. The cost ranges from $160 to $1400.

VENDORS

The names and phone numbers of some manufacturers of electronic switching devices are listed below. Call them for their product specifications and current price list:

Fifth Generation Systems	(800) 225-2775
Server Technology	1-800-835-1515
Buffalo Products	(800) 345-2356
Black Box Corp.	(412) 746-5530
Crosspoint Systems	(800) 232-7729
Digital Products	(800) 243-2333
Extended Systems	(208) 322-7163
Rose Electronics	(713) 933-7673
Western Telematic	(800) 854-7226
Quadram	(404) 564-5566

Listed below are the names and telephone numbers of some dot matrix printer makers:

Star Micronics	(212) 986-6770
Advanced Matrix Technology	(805) 499-8741
Alps America	(800) 828-2557
Brother International	(201) 981-0300
C. Itoh Digital Products	(213) 327-2110
Canon U.S.A.	(516) 488-6700
Citizen American	(213) 453-0614
Dataproducts Corp.	(603) 673-9100
Datasouth Computer Corp.	(800) 222-4528
Epson America	(213) 539-9140
Fujitsu America	(408) 946-8777
Genicom Corp.	(703) 949-1000
IBM Corp.	(800) 426-2468
Infoscribe	(800) 233-4442
JDL Inc.	(805) 495-3451
Mannesmann Tally	(206) 251-5500
NEC Information Systems	(800) 343-4418
Newbury Data Inc.	(213) 372-3775

Nissho Information Systems	(714) 952-8700
Okidata	(800) 654-3282
Olympia	(201) 722-7000
Output Technology	(800) 468-8788
Panasonic Industrial Co.	(201) 348-7000
Printronix	(714) 863-1900
Seikosha America	(201) 529-4655
Tandy/Radio Shack	(817) 390-3011
Texas Instruments	(800) 527-3500
Toshiba America	(714) 730-5000

Here are the telephone numbers of a few laser printer companies with models costing less than $3000:

Epson	(800) 421-5426
Hewlett-Packard	(800) 367-4772
Okidata	(609) 235-2600
QMS	(205) 633-4300
Ricoh	(201) 892-2000

11

Desktop Publishing

The desktop publishing (DTP) era began in January, 1985 with the introduction of Apple's LaserWriter and Aldus Corporation's PageMaker software. Credit Paul Brainerd of Aldus with creating the term *desktop publishing*.

The Apple LaserWriter was more expensive than other laser printers on the market at that time, but with the PageMaker software, the Macintosh could mix several different fonts and graphics, and shift, rotate, format, and print them out through the LaserWriter, exactly as seen on the screen. No PC, XT, or AT could do what the Macintosh could do.

One reason the Apple LaserWriter was so much more expensive than other laser printers was that it was equipped with a controller board and software from Adobe Systems called PostScript, a page description language (PDL). The PDL acts as an interpreter for the received output from the computer. It causes the laser printer to print out an exact copy of the page that has been created on the screen.

Without a PDL, most laser printers are set up much like monitors. The adapter that drives the monitor has all 256 characters stored in different addresses on the board. When you type an A or B, that character is replicated from a stored image and sent to the screen. There are usually only one or two sizes of characters stored on these adapter boards, so those are the only sizes that can normally be displayed on the screen.

If you want a different size character or font, you usually have to use some sort of graphics program to create it.

Laser printers behave much the same way. They come with some memory that can act as a buffer and two or three different font sizes. You can plug different cartridges into some printers for different fonts. To print graphics, they must be driven by special software and hardware that is analogous to the graphics adapters and software needed to create graphics on a monitor display.

A standard page is 8.5 inches wide and 11 inches long. The laser printers have a resolution of 300 dots per inch. This yields 8,415,000 dots that can appear on a printed page. A PDL, along with quite a lot of memory, controls where these individual dots are placed.

PostScript, the PDL used on the Apple LaserWriter, was one of the reasons DTP became such a hit. Several other laser printer companies immediately began developing their own PDLs. They were called by different names, like Imagen's Document Description Language (DDL), Hewlett-Packard's HP Graphics Language (HPGL), and Xerox's Interpress.

The laser printer industry is no different than the dot-matrix printer industry regarding standards. It has none. Software developers had to create drivers that would work with all PDLs on the market.

Recently, IBM has indicated it will be entering the DTP business and has chosen PostScript. This endorsement should serve to create a standard of some sort.

PostScript controllers are expensive. In many cases they may cost twice as much as a whole laser printer. The Laser Connection, Box 850296, Mobile, AL 36685, offers a PostScript controller for the Hewlett-Packard Laserjet and other laser printers that use the Canon engine, for a mere $2995. See Fig. 11-1.

The Laser Connection is a subsidiary of the QMS Corporation, which manufactures Kiss and Big Kiss laser printers. The Laser Connection publishes a catalog that lists several other products for laser printers and adjuncts of DTP.

One product handled by the Laser Connection is the Tall Tree JLASER RAM board. This board can plug into a PC, XT, or AT and add 2 megabytes of memory to your system. Some DTP software, such as Ventura, Dr. Halo, PC Paintbrush +, and several other programs, can use this bit-mapped memory to control the laser printout. The JLASER RAM board with 2 megabytes lists for about $1300. It is not nearly as powerful as PostScript or the other PDLs and is not a good substitute for a PDL.

At this writing (July, 1987) there are several companies who are designing clones of the PostScript board. Using VLSI technology, these

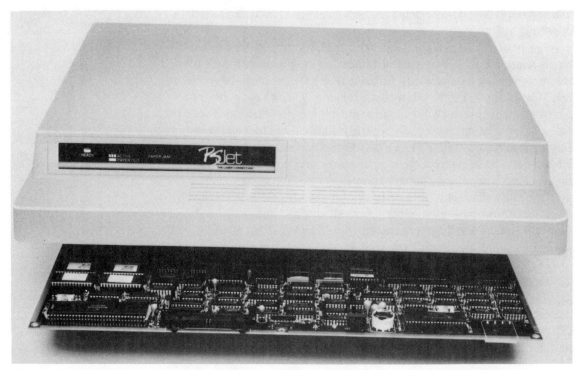

Fig. 11-1. A PS Jet laser printer controller board with a PDL language. (Photo courtesy of PS Jet Corp.)

clones will be built on a board that plugs into a slot in a PC, XT, or AT. You can bet they will cost a lot less than $3000, especially after they are cloned by the Far East companies. The cost of DTP should have gone way down by the time you read this.

THE PROLIFERATION OF DTP

It didn't take long for IBM and the MS-DOS world to realize what a fantastic tool desktop publishing could be. It has been estimated that the DTP industry will be worth 6 billion dollars by 1990.

Companies could now publish in-house their own manuals, documents, management directives, and training aids. They could print professional-looking proposals in just hours. They no longer had to send pasted-up material out to a print shop, wait a week for it to come back, and then find out that it had several errors. They could change or edit any documents in minutes, then print out a clean copy. They found that DTP was great for newsletters, pamphlets, brochures, and even books.

Many software companies began developing DTP programs for DOS. Dozens of software packages are now available for PCs, XTs and ATs, costing from $200 to $900. Some very high-level programs cost as much as $8000.

One reason DTP using the Macintosh became so popular was the mouse which allows you to point at a menu or item and manipulate it. Microsoft Windows and a mouse makes a DOS machine almost easy to use. Most of the DTP software works within the Windows environment.

One advantage the DOS environment had over the Macintosh was the fact that large monitors could be easily attached to DOS machines. The Macintosh came with a small monochrome screen, and it was very difficult to attach a larger monitor, or add extra memory or a large hard disk.

The open architecture of IBM compatibles allowed the addition of extra memory, many different boards, or large hard disks. Apple realized this; when the DOS world started nibbling away at what had been exclusively Apple's DTP territory, they came out with their own MS-DOS-compatible, open-architecture Macintosh II.

The Macintosh II is a good machine, but it is still priced about the same as the high-end IBM AT. You can assemble an 80286 clone for about half the cost of a Macintosh. Incidentally, there are about 400,000 original small-screen Macintoshes in existence. There are over 10 million PCs, XTs, and compatibles in use. Guess which type of computer will have the most DTP hardware and software availability in the next few months?

WHAT IS DESIRED IN A DTP PROGRAM

You want the program to accept text and data from your word processor, spreadsheets, and data bases. You would like to place text of all sizes and varieties on the screen. You want to be able to place the text in columns and use kerning to space words and characters for the purpose of justification. You would also like automatic hyphenation and pagination.

You want to place graphs, charts, and symbols on the screen, along with photos and drawings, and be able to move, rotate, crop, reduce or enhance them. And you also want a WYSIWYG (What You See Is What You Get) system that will print out exactly what is laid out on the screen.

COST OF A DTP SYSTEM

The cost of a system depends on what you want it to do.
Here are some of the things you will need for a basic system:

Item	Cost
A computer, PC, XT or an AT with at least 640 K	$400-1000
A 40 megabyte hard disk	500-1000
A monitor, large, high resolution, EGA adapter	1000-3000

Software, word processor	$ 200-400
Software, for DTP	200-900
Scanner, for OCR and Image input	1000-4000
A mouse	60-120
A modem	200-500
A laser printer	1500-6000
Total	$5060-16920

There can be over $11,000 difference depending on what you want. Let's look at each item:

You could actually get by with a PC or XT. A basic clone without a monitor would only cost about $400, but it would be slower than an 80286. If you have more time than money you could save quite a bit, but you probably won't be too happy.

You could probably get by with a smaller hard disk, but, again, you probably won't be too happy with anything less. With an RLL controller, you should be able to find a 40-megabyte drive for not much more than $500.

The monitor should have a large screen in monochrome or high-resolution color. See Fig. 11-2. Wyse Technology sells a high-resolution, 15-inch monochrome monitor with an adapter for $999. However, many DTP software programs need the Windows environment in order to use the mouse, and Windows needs a color monitor and EGA.

You might think that you wouldn't need both a word processor and desktop publishing software. The DTP software can let you enter text, edit, and re-arrange it, but its primary function is to allow page formatting on the screen of your monitor. It is much better to use a word processor, like WordStar4, to create text files. These files can then be copied to the DTP program for page layout and formatting.

It is almost essential that you have a scanner that can read both text and images and put them in the computer. There are some companies, such as Canon, who are manufacturing scanners that are also facsimile machines. Facsimile machines have been around awhile, but this device can scan images or text and send it to the computer or across the country over ordinary telephone lines.

One of the biggest reasons the Macintosh became so popular was that the mouse made using the computer much easier to learn. A mouse is essential to moving the cursor around in "cutting and pasting" to format a page.

A modem is necessary to send or receive data from other computers. It is possible to even send DTP formatted data over a modem to a printer at some other location.

Fig. 11-2. A high resolution monitor for desktop publishing. (Photo courtesy of Micro Display Systems.)

It is possible to buy a laser printer for about $1500, but it would only have about 256 K of memory and no more than two fonts. It would print text very well, but it would not be able to print graphics or a variety of fonts and text sizes. More fonts and memory may cost up to $2000 more. A PDL controller for graphics might cost $3000 more, so $6000 for a DTP laser printer is not a bad price.

USING A DOT-MATRIX PRINTER

It is possible to use a good 24-pin dot-matrix printer to do low-end DTP. You will not have the same quality as the high-end laser-produced material, but if you are on a tight budget, it might be a good alternative. Some newer word-processing programs, such as WordStar4, PFS:First Choice, and others, can do a decent job controlling the printout.

The LeBaugh Software Company, (800) 532-2844, produces a program called LePrint that will allow page-formatted data to be printed on laser or dot-matrix printers. They have several versions costing $175 to $325.

Plummer Research, (415) 324-8160, publishes PAGEr, a $49.95 program that allows page composition for dot-matrix printers. It can read ASCII files into columns and has line, arrow, and shape drawing capabilities for diagrams and forms.

SOURCES

Almost every major computer magazine has at least one article on DTP in every issue, but the people who publish *PC World* have created a bi-monthly magazine called *PUBLISH!*. It is dedicated solely to the DTP industry. (Its address is listed in Chapter 14.)

If you are interested in setting up a DTP system, I recommend that you compare several alternatives. If possible, visit the showrooms of several vendors and see an actual demonstration. At COMDEX or Computer Faires, you can see several systems being demonstrated, sometimes right alongside each other.

Several large companies are now offering turnkey systems. They provide all the components needed for a complete system. You just tell them what you want your system to do and they will assemble the system for you. You will have to pay a bit extra for their expertise in selecting your system. If you don't have the time to investigate the many options available, it may be worth the extra money.

NEW JARGON

The DTP industry has created a whole new language. Here is a short lexicon of some of those arcane and mysterious terms.

alignment—How the text is lined up on a page or a column. It can be aligned flush right, center, flush left or justified on both sides.

baseline—The line on which the characters sit, except for those with descenders like g, j, p, q, and y. Some characters have ascenders like b, d, f, h, k, 1, and t. The "X height" of a letter is proportionate to lower-case x, which has neither ascenders nor descenders.

bit map—A graphic image formed by a matrix of dots.

blue pencil—Many photocopy machines cannot detect certain types of blue, so the copy can be marked up with these pens or pencils. The marks will not show up when the copy is printed out.

clipboard—A holding place for temporarily storing text or graphics.

crop—To trim the edges of a photo or graphics image to make it fit in an allotted space for artistic purposes or to emphasize a certain portion.

dialog box—A window or full-screen display that pops up in response to a command.

font—A complete set of characters, all of the same type face and point size, for instance, 10-point Courier or 12-point italic.
footer—One or more lines of text that appear at the bottom of each page.

generic font—Characters displayed on the screen that may not be the same as those to be printed out.
greeking—Symbolic bars or boxes that show where text would be on a line, but not the actual alphanumeric character.

header—One or two lines of text that appear at the top of each page.
H and J—Short for hyphenation and justification. Some programs can do these things automatically using a large dictionary.

icon—A graphic representation of a file or a command that is displayed on the screen. A mouse can be pointed to an icon and clicked and the command will be performed. An example is the trashcan used on Apple programs. When this icon is invoked, characters or blocks are deleted.

kerning—The variation of space between letters for visual effect and justification.

leaders—Dotted or dashed lines that can be defined for tab settings.
leading—Pronounced "ledding." In printing, a *lead* is a flat piece of lead that is placed between the baselines of text to separate them. The width of the lead is expressed in points. This determines the line spacing. Some DTP programs can vary the leading (or spacing) between lines.

orphans and widows—The first line of a paragraph is called an orphan when it is the last line on a page and is separated from the rest of the paragraph by a page break. The last line of a paragraph is called a widow when it is forced onto a new page by a page break.

phototypesetting—Producing a page image on photosensitive paper so that it can be printed out on a Linotronic typesetter. Many of the major DTP programs are capable of interfacing with a Linotronic typesetter.

pica—A unit of measure equal to ⅙ of an inch or 12 points.

point—Smallest unit of typographic measurement. There are 72 points to an inch, or 6 picas.

serif—Certain fonts have a small line at the top or bottom of the letters. For instance, look at the lines at the top of a capital W, or the foot of a capital T. *Sans serif* would be certain types of fonts that do not have the serifs.

vertical justification—The ability to adjust the leading or spacing between lines of text in point increments so that a column can fill a whole space. It can be used to control widows and orphans to some extent.

WYSIWYG—Pronounced "wizzywig." An acronym for What-You-See-Is-What-You-Get. Many better DTP programs and word processors let you see onscreen what the printout will look like.

12

Local Area Networks

Local area networks (LAN) are an even greater phenomenon than desktop publishing, but networks have been around a bit longer. Xerox was first to use LAN in 1978 when they developed Ethernet. However, LAN really didn't take off until 1983, when the era of the personal computer really began. Since that time, there seems to be at least one article on networking in every issue of every major computer magazine.

Many of those articles speciously emphasize the simplicity and ease of installing a network system. Unless you know what you are doing and are very careful, a network system can be a nightmare.

I don't mean to discourage anyone from using these fantastic tools. Some of them are easy to install and maintain, but these simpler systems are usually rather limited in what they can do. Most of the more sophisticated systems need professional installation and maintenance.

LACK OF STANDARDS

One problem again is standardization. There have been some achievements, but not nearly enough. There are still a few companies, like Wang, who have their own proprietary network systems that will not work with any other network.

The Ethernet system came first and presented a standard that could have made networking a lot easier if IBM had joined them. Nonetheless, IBM set up their own Token Ring system.

The International Standards Organization (ISO) has tried to establish the Open System Interconnection (OSI). This is a standard that addresses physical types, transmission, and protocols. This standard has not been widely embraced.

General Motors uses many computers, CAD/CAM/CIM, robots, and computerized machinery. It has had great difficulty interfacing their various components. GM suggested a set of standards called Manufacturing Automation Protocol (MAP). Several large firms have joined General Motors in pushing for such standards, but they have not been very successful.

Again, I am not trying to discourage you—I doubt you will ever be faced with the problems General Motors has. Networking can be a valuable and productive tool. But if you plan on installing a fairly large system, you probably should research, comparison shop, and perhaps hire a reputable consultant before spending a lot of money.

WHAT A LAN IS

A LAN consists of two or more computers tied together so that they share files. Most systems require a plug-in board, shown in Fig. 12-1, and software to drive them. Some companies manufacture boards or hardware only, some make both hardware and software, and some make only software. Novell is one of the best known companies that provides only software. Their software will operate with the hardware of dozens of other manufacturers.

Quite often one computer will act as the server for one or more workstations. A workstation is shown in Fig. 12-2. For instance, an 80286 computer could have a 40-megabyte, or even 240-megabytes, hard disk system. The hard disk could store records of the company's customers, their account numbers, their addresses, and other pertinent information. This database might also include the company's inventory. It could also include accounts payable, accounts receivable, employee payroll information, company assets and liabilities, computerized forecasts, budgets, and other financial information.

The server hard disk could have several software programs, such as WordStar4, for word processing; dBASE III PLUS, for data base users; SuperCalc4, for financial and spread sheet needs; and several other application-specific programs. This software and the files on the hard disk could be available to anyone with a workstation tied to the system.

Printers sit idle much of the time. It is not cost-effective to have a

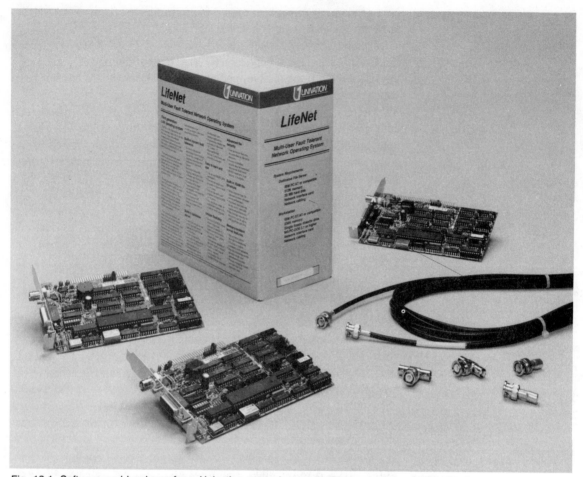

Fig. 12-1. Software and hardware for a Univation network system. (Photo courtesy of Univation.)

printer at each work station. The server could be attached to one or more printers. These printers would then be available to anyone on the network and be much better utilized.

A server could also hold records of work schedules, overhead costs, and statistical trends. It might have software for computer-aided design/computer-aided manufacturing/computer integrated manufacturing (CAD/CAM/CIM). It might also be used to design and implement programs for numerically-controlled (NC) machines.

The network could use a bar-code system to keep track of the time each employee spent on a job. A laser printer could be used to print bar-coded work orders and labels. A bar-coded label could be attached to each part. Each employee could have a bar code on his badge with his name.

Fig. 12-2. A 3COM local area network station. (Photo courtesy of 3COM Corp.)

When he begins a job, he would use a scanner to read the label on the part, the bar code on the work order and the bar code on his badge. When this employee finished the operation he was performing, he would again scan the bar codes and log off. The computer would then, for example, have a record of the time charged against the job, where the part was in the production cycle, and where it was physically located.

Many stores and small businesses can benefit greatly by installing bar-code systems. A videotape rental store in my area has put bar-code labels on all their videotapes. They have also made up a small bar code for each regular customer. They then placed the small bar code on the back of one of each customer's credit cards. With this system, the store can process the check-out and check-in of tapes in a few seconds.

There are thousands of other ways that network systems can be used for greater productivity and resource sharing, and there are thousands of different types of networks.

A MEDICAL OFFICE SYSTEM

I have a friend who is a medical doctor with a fairly good practice in a small town. He employs a nurse and a receptionist. The receptionist answers the phones, schedules the patients, and makes the coffee. The nurse aids the doctor and keeps the patients' records.

I visited him one day and mentioned that he could use a computer system. He said, ''Great. Set one up for me.''

I had no idea what I was getting into. I first began looking for medical office software. There really isn't too much available. Most of what is available costs too much—I looked at some programs that had list prices of $5000 to $6000. These programs merely scheduled patients, posted bills, completed insurance forms, and maintained a small block of the patient's history. The patient history portion usually had a listing of drugs given and procedures performed, for billing purposes.

I finally settled on a software package from Charles Mann Associates. In the brochures that I had received, it looked great. It had provisions for scheduling, billing, accounting, and patient history, and it cost a little less than $2000.

I was quite disappointed when I got the package and found that the manuals had been written in 1983 and had not been substantially updated since. The instructions for installation mentioned floppies and a 5-megabyte hard disk. I don't know anybody who still uses a 5-megabyte hard disk. The installation instructions were dispersed throughout the first 40 pages. The manuals were very poorly written. I seriously considered sending it back before I even looked at the software, but I didn't have much of an alternative. Besides, I figured that if the company had been around since 1983, they must have had time to iron all of the bugs out of their programs.

The software was written in compiled BASIC. My first problem was that they offered two versions. One runs only the IBM, using IBM ROM BASIC. Their brochure wasn't explicit on this point, so I got the wrong version and it would not run at all with GW-BASIC. When I got the other version and tried to install and run it, all kinds of error messages popped up. There was no explanation of the error messages in the manual. I spent hours on long-distance telephone calls before I finally got it up and running.

The doctor wanted a network of three computers: one for the receptionist, one for the nurse and one for his office desk. We decided to use an 80286 with a 30-megabyte hard disk for the server and two XT clones for the workstations.

I really didn't know too much about network systems, so I let a super salesman talk me into buying a Gateway system for a discount price of only $2200. This didn't seem too bad, because most of the more sophisticated systems cost about $1000 for the server and about the same per node (or workstation).

When I got the package, it had three boards with several DIP switches on each one, nine manuals, and 14 floppy disks. See Fig. 12-3. The manuals, the switch settings on the boards, and the order of the installation of the floppy disks were all inter-related.

I found that all the floppy disks had to be DISKCOPYed onto backup copies. Several disks had hidden files that could not be copied with a simple COPY *.* command.

Fig. 12-3. In rear, the nine manuals and 14 disks that came with the first system I ordered. In left foreground are the single manual and floppy disk of the Invisinet Company. It used the IBM PC Network software.

During installation, the program is copied from the floppy onto the hard disk, then its files are converted, compressed, and contorted. It takes 15 to 20 minutes just to load a floppy disk. One of the manuals said it takes from six to eight hours to load the system. I tried for a week. I would get it all loaded, then run it and get an error message and have to start all over again. If every step is not done in exactly the proper sequence, it won't run. I consider myself fairly intelligent. I am proud that I am a member of Mensa. This system was completely beyond me. I finally gave up and ordered a system from Invisinet.

Invisinet was much less expensive than Gateway. It required a board for each system (shown in Fig. 12-4), a single disk of software drivers, and a small, staple-bound manual. It could be controlled by several different network-system software packages, such as Novell, 3COM or IBM's PC Network. I chose IBM because it was the least expensive, at $125 per node. The Invisinet boards, shown in Fig. 12-2, cost $249 each. Each node of this system cost about $375. Figure 12-5 shows all three of the nodes running after only an hour of installation.

The doctor's office is about 200 miles from where I live. I drove up and installed it in one weekend. One immediately apparent problem was that the twisted-pair cables had to be run through walls and across a hallway. The building had a concrete floor and did not have a false ceiling,

Fig. 12-4. An Invisinet plug-in card for LANs.

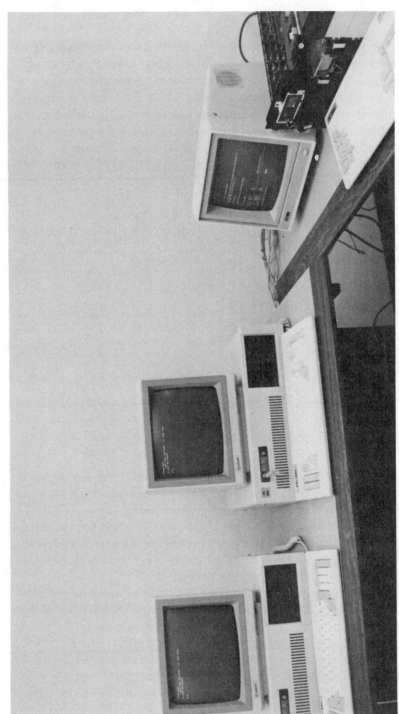

Fig. 12-5. The medical office network up and running.

so I had to staple the wires up and around the door frames, drill holes through the walls, and staple directly to the ceiling tile.

After I got it all hooked together, one of the nodes did not work. The system uses telephone wire with miniature snap-in connectors (now standard on all telephones). I determined that one of the miniature connectors had a bad crimp. I went down to Radio Shack and bought a standard telephone-extension line with connectors on each end. It worked great.

Neither the doctor nor his staff had ever used a computer before. I assembled several elementary books and a couple of tutorials. I have had to spend hours on the phone helping them with simple problems, but the system is working fine and they are all fast learners. The doctor and his staff are very happy.

He is especially happy with the cost of the system. Because he is a very close friend, I charged him exactly what it cost me. Here is a breakdown:

Medical and Accounting Software	$1996
1 80286 computer, 1 M memory	1100
1 30-M hard disk & controller	550
2 Turbo XTs, 640 K, 1 floppy	1260
2 12-inch monochrome monitors	198
1 14-inch monochrome monitor	149
3 monitor drivers	240
1 copy DOS 3.2 with GW BASIC	75
3 Invisinet boards @ $249 ea.	747
3 copies IBM-PC Net @ $125 ea.	375
1 Star NB25-15 dot-matrix printer	655
Total	$7345

A comparable system installed by a consultant or turnkey-systems company might cost twice this much. A small system like this is ideal for doctors, dentists, lawyers, and small businesses.

There are other systems, even less expensive, that use the serial ports of the computer to link five or six computers together, and there are much more expensive systems that require very large hard disks, co-axial cables and complex operating software.

If you need a network system, I suggest that you subscribe to a LAN magazine. (See Chapter 14 for a list of magazines.) Study some of the articles on LANs that appear in other computer magazines.

When the OS/2 operating system becomes available, the 80286 will be capable of operating as a multiuser station, operating in the protected mode. This capability alone is worth the money and effort to upgrade your old PC or XT with a Baby AT board or to put together a 286 system from scratch.

13

Recommended Software

DOS 3.3 is now available, but it doesn't do that much more than DOS 3.2. If you have DOS 2.1 and decide to move up to 3.2 or 3.3, you must completely back up your hard disk and reformat it with the newer DOS. The operating system is stored on reserved sectors and tracks on the hard disk, and SYS must be the first thing loaded on a clean disk. Each newer version is bigger than the last one, so there is not enough space in the reserved sectors for 3.2 or 3.3 on a disk that has been formatted for 2.1. You can go downward with no problem (copy DOS 3.2 over 3.3, or 2.1 over either of them), but there's little reason to.

I am not sure DOS 3.3 is worth the extra money. It was written by IBM, and there have been some reports that it causes problems when installed on clones. You might be better off waiting for OS/2.

Other than the operating system, there are five basic types of software you should have to make your computer more productive. These are word processors, data bases, spreadsheets, utilities, and disk management programs.

WORD PROCESSORS

There are many good word processors. I use word processing more than any other software. I have several word-processor packages, but

I started out with WordStar in 1983, and that is the one I use most often. There were several things that I didn't like about the original WordStar, so I patched and customized it.

I was happy when they released WordStar4. Micropro added over 125 features and made WordStar4 very easy to change and customize. Through DOS commands from within the WS4 directory, you can type WSCHANGE, and up pop several menus that allow you to change the clolors of the WordStar 4 menus, redefine the function keys, and change printers.

While editing a file, press CONTROL QM, and up pops a window which lets you perform almost any math function you would find on an ordinary calculator.

ESCAPE causes a SHORTHAND window to pop up. It has several predefined MACROS, but you can develop your own. For instance, if you are writing a letter, instead of typing the date, you can press ESCAPE, then SHIFT and @ and the day's date prints out at the cursor. I write a lot of letters, so one of the first things I did was create a MACRO for closing and for my return address.

When I write a letter I use macros for the date, my closing and my address. After I have completed a letter, which is usually a single page, I force a page break with a .PA command. I then use Control KN for column block mode, move the cursor to my return address, press SHIFT F9 to mark the beginning of a block, and move to the end of my address, pressing SHIFT F10 to mark the end of the block. I then move the cursor to the top left corner of page 2 and press SHIFT F8 to copy the return address. I move to the top of the letter and use SHIFT F9 and SHIFT F10 to mark the beginning and end of the recipient's address. I then move the cursor to the end of the file with Control END, move down 10 spaces, tab over to column 50, and press SHIFT F8 to copy the recipient's address. When I print my letter, I have the printer pause between pages. I take out the first page, insert the envelope in the printer, and press P. The envelope is automatically addressed. This sounds like it would be a lot of work, but it really isn't. It is much faster and easier than using a typewriter to address the envelope.

The new WordStar also saves margin settings with files. When you re-edit a file, you don't have to reset your margins. I would have liked for it to save the line format commands also, but it doesn't. For instance, for my articles and this book, I have to double space and use an unjustified right margin. I used WSCHANGE to make the ragged-right margin come up as a default, but each time I call up a file, I have to reset the line spacing to double. I could change that too, if I used the patching menu, but it is not that much trouble to change the spacing. Just press CONTROL O S 2 and RETURN.

The spelling checker will now let you check the word at the cursor anytime by pressing SHIFT and F4. You may press CONTROL Q O and type a word, and WordStar4 will tell you if it is spelled correctly. SHIFT F3 checks spelling in the whole file.

The old spelling checker gave a count of misspelled words and the total number of words in a file. This was very helpful because editors always want to know how many words you have used. The new spelling checker does not give the number of words, but there is a WC (for Word Count) program that can be run from DOS that counts the lines, characters, and words, and lists the file name.

As with the original WordStar, you can run any DOS command from the opening menu by typing R and the command. I use the R command quite often when I want to erase my old backup files. I just type R, then at the D >, erase *.BAK and RETURN. The changes and additions to WordStar help make life easier for me and I am delighted with it.

Word Finder

Word Finder is an excellent thesaurus program. I bought it when it first came out and installed it with my old WordStar. It now comes free with WordStar4. I have a couple copies of *Roget's Thesaurus*, but it is inconvenient to have to stop and look up a word. It is so much easier to place the cursor at a word, press ALT 1, and see a list of synonyms pop up on the screen. I can then move the cursor to any one of the synonyms that I want to use, press ENTER or RETURN, and that word will replace the one in my file.

RightWriter

RightWriter is a program that takes a document and analyzes it. It checks for grammatical errors and suggests ways to make the document more powerful. It checks for unusual words and jargon and gives a readability index. The index is based on the complexity of the sentences, length of the words, and use of adjectives and adverbs. the readability index figure is the approximate grade level of education needed to understand the writing.

Some people can spell almost anything and have a great command of the language, yet they might not be very bright. Conversely, there are those who are very intelligent, but cannot spell or write very well. This could jeopardize a good career. If you have trouble writing, you need a word processor with a good spelling checker, a thesaurus, and perhaps a program like RightWriter.

DATABASES

One of the least expensive and easiest to use databases is called askSAM. This strange name is an acronym for Access Stored Knowledge via Symbolic Access Method. It is a text-oriented, database management system and is not necessarily structured. However, it may be structured with explicit fields. It is very flexible and surprisingly easy to use.

DATAEASE is another database that is not necessarily structured but is much larger and more complex than askSAM. It is easy to use and to learn but is more expensive than askSAM.

The most popular of all databases is dBASE III. The latest version is easier to learn than the original dBASE II, but it can still be very frustrating at times. Genifer is a program that can be used with dBASE III to create your own application programs. With Genifer's menus, even an inexperienced person can develop a useful, bug-free program in a short time. The experienced programmer can also save time and create better programs with Genifer. Genifer can use WordStar or almost any other editor to create dBASE III programs.

SPREADSHEETS

SuperCalc has always been one of the better spreadsheet programs. The present version, SuperCalc4, has many more features and functions than Lotus 1-2-3, but for some reason it has never enjoyed the popularity of Lotus 1-2-3. SuperCalc4 is not copy protected. Lotus is almost paranoid about its copy protection; it is one of the few major software packages that is still copy protected.

There are many varied applications for spreadsheets: budgets and forecasting, sales and profit projections, investment portfolios, estate and financial planning and management, comparative investment analysis, personnel records, inventory records, job-cost estimates, balance sheet and income statement preparation, cash-flow analysis, graphing and chart-making, and the manipulation of any numeric data that requires reports, updating, and computations.

Basically, spreadsheets use cells to hold data and formulae. If the data is changed in one cell and data in other cells depend on that cell, the data in the other cells will be recalculated accordingly.

SuperCalc4 is quite versatile in that it can import and export the files of Lotus 1-2-3, dBASE II and III, programs written in BASIC, and several other sources. It has a very good manual which has a tutorial for beginners. In its category, it is definitely one of the better programs.

UTILITIES

The Paul Mace Utilities program is inexpensive software that can pay for itself many times over. It can unfragment a hard disk. That alone is worth the price of the package, but it can do several other very useful things.

It can look at a hard disk and detect problems that might be lurking there. If it finds a spot on the disk that appears to be going bad, it can remove the data and write it to a safer spot.

There are several programs that will un-erase a file, but Mace will actually recover the files from a hard disk that has been reformatted.

Most of the Mace operations are performed by one of the function keys. F1 is an online help function. F3 diagnoses the hard disk and looks for bad sectors; F5 will remedy the situation, marking off the bad sectors so that they will be locked out. F6 can squeeze, sort, and remove deleted directories and close up spaces. F7 is the condense operation that unfragments the disk. Depending on the size of the disk and the number of files, it might take more than an hour to run. F8 creates a duplicate copy of the boot sector each time the machine is booted up. It stores this copy near the end of the disk. Ordinarily, if the boot sector or file allocation table is damaged, there is no way to recover any of your files. With this backup, Mace does it easily. Mace is a utility that every hard disk owner should have.

DISK MANAGEMENT

QDOSII is a program that lets you look at all your directories, pick any one directory, look at the files in that directory, and, if they are in ASCII, view them, tag them, copy them to another directory or disk, or erase them. It lets you look at hidden files, change their attributes to un-hide them, and make hidden files out of normal files. You can also use it to rename, search for, or move files. It is a very handy tool.

1DIR + is a hard disk manager that is similar to QDOS II, but it offers more functions. It can sort a directory by name, extension, date or size. It has a pop-up notepad for making notes while in another program and a batch builder that helps you make batch files. It makes generous use of menus and windows. It comes with a spiral-bound manual that has about 200 pages of well-written information.

WINDOWS

Windows is a graphics-oriented operating environment for DOS. It allows you to work with several programs at once and can switch from one to another. It allows you to use icons, drop-down menus, and dialog boxes. In other words, it makes the DOS environment more like the Macintosh world.

There are several software programs that have already been written to run with Windows. IBM has chosen it for the OS/2 system, although IBM will call it their *Presentation Manager*. IBM spent lots of time and money on a similar program called TopView, but it has not been too popular. So IBM bit the bullet and selected Windows.

Windows is relatively inexpensive. It lists for $99. I have seen it advertised for $60. The manual alone, which is about 400 pages long, is worth the price of the package.

14

Sources

The computer industry is extremely volatile. New products and technologies are introduced daily. To keep up with the latest in the computer business, subscribe to the magazines listed below. These magazines publish articles on all the latest developments. Many of these magazines try to find a niche and distinguish themselves from the others. Several new magazines have been introduced in the last few months to address new technologies. Examples are *Publish!* for desktop publishing and *LAN* for local area networks.

All of the magazines have something to offer. They are educational, informative, and well worth the money. Some of them are free of charge.

MAIL ORDER

These magazines are full of ads for computer components and systems. You can use the ads to comparison shop without leaving home. You can plan your system and have a fairly good idea of how much it will cost. If you don't live where there are lots of computer stores, you can order your system through the mail. Most of the larger mail-order stores have developed a fairly good reputation for delivering as advertised. A recent article in *PC Week Magazine* said that about $2.1 billion worth of PC equipment would be sold through the mails during 1987.

SOME MAIL ORDER CONSIDERATIONS

You should read the ads very carefully. Some of them show a complete system and a low price, but the actual ad might not offer all that is shown in the picture. If the price looks too good to be true, it probably is.

You should have a fairly good idea of what you are buying. Some copywriters get carried away, and the description that they provide might not exactly match the product.

You should have a fairly good idea of the cost of the item. Many ads are made up a month in advance, so prices could have changed since the ad was placed. Call your vendor to verify the price and model, and get as many other details as possible. Ask about shipping costs. Shipping and handling could make the purchase more costly than buying locally.

Many companies will take an order over the telephone and allow you to charge it to your charge card. You should be aware that the Federal Trade Commission offers some protection if you order by mail, but they can't help you if the order is placed by telephone.

MAGAZINES

Here is a list of magazines you should consider subscribing to. This is only a partial listing; there are many other good magazines on the market.

Computer Shopper
407 S. Washington Av.
Titusville, FL 32796

MicroTimes Magazine
5951 Canning St.
Oakland, CA 94609

PC World Magazine
501 Second St.
San Francisco, CA 94107

PC Clones
5211 S. Washington Av.
Titusville, FL 32780

PC Magazine
One Park Av.
New York, NY 10016

Personal Computing
10 Mulholland Dr.
Hasbrouck Hts., NJ 07604

Business Software
P.O. Box 27975
San Diego, CA 92128

PC Tech Journal
P.O. Box 2968
Boulder, CO 80321

Byte Magazine
70 Main St.
Peterborough, NH 03458

Publish!
P.O. Box 55400
Boulder, CO 80321-5400

LAN
12 West 21 Street
New York, NY 10010

Computer Graphic
Harris Publications
Dept. CGM
1115 S. Broadway
New York, NY 10010

CD-ROM Review
P.O. Box 921
Farmingdale, NY 11737-9621

FREE MAGAZINES

PC Week
P.O. Box 5920
Cherry Hill, NJ 08034

Computer Currents
5720 Hollis St.
Emeryville, CA 94608

InfoWorld
1060 Marsh Rd.
Menlo Park, CA 94025

Computer Systems News
600 Community Dr.
Manhasset, NY 11030

Information Week
600 Community Dr.
Manhasset, NY 11030

PC Resource
P.O. Box 950
Farmingdale, NY 11737-9650

Computer Living
5795 Tyndall Av.
Riverdale, NY 10471

Texas Computing
17818 Davenport, #119
Dallas, TX 75252

The Inputer
P.O. Box 20410
Montgomery, AL 36177

Computer + Software News
P.O. Box 3119
Grand Central Station
New York, NY 10164-0659

Mini-Micro Systems
P.O. Box 5051
Denver, CO 80217-9872

Computer Products
P.O. Box 14000
Dover, NJ 07801-9990

Circulation Dept.
Machine Design
Penton Publishing
1100 Superior Av.
Cleveland, OH 44114

ID Systems
174 Concord St.
Peterborough, NH 03458

The subscription price of a magazine usually does not cover the costs of publication and distribution. Most magazines depend almost entirely on advertisers for their existence. The more subscribers a magazine has, the more it can charge for its ads. They can attract a lot more subscribers if the magazine is free.

To get a free subscription, you must write to the magazine for an application form. The form will ask several questions which are meant to establish a marketing profile of their readers. Many of these magazines also make money by selling this specialized mailing list to direct mail advertisers.

Some time ago, I filled out a qualification application form for one of the free magazines, but I never received it. I happened to meet its editor at one of the computer shows. I complained that I had never received the magazine; his reply was that I probably had not lied enough on the form to qualify.

I am not suggesting you lie when you fill out the qualifying forms, but unless you work for a large company and have lots of purchasing influence, it might help if you exaggerate a little.

MicroTimes Magazine, listed above, is distributed free through computer stores and at computer shows throughout California. It is an excellent magazine. You can also have it delivered to your home for just $12 a year.

The above list is not nearly complete. Hundreds of trade magazines are free to qualified subscribers. The Cahners Company alone publishes 32 different trade magazines. Many of the trade magazines are highly technical and narrowly specialized.

MAIL ORDER MAGAZINES

Some magazines are strictly mail order. One surprising example comes from 47th Street Photo. In the past, they dealt mostly in camera equipment. I recently ordered some camera equipment from them and am now on their mailing list. They publish a monthly catalog. The May issue had 226 pages, and over half of them were for computers and computer-related products. Their catalog has a cover price of $2.95, but once you have ordered something from them, you are on their mailing list and will receive it free. The address is:

47 St. Photo
36 East 19th St.
New York, NY 10003
(212) 260-4410

Another magazine that is filled with ads is *Nuts & Volts.* It is given away free at most computer swaps, but you can subscribe to it for $10 per year or $50 for a lifetime subscription. The address is:

Nuts & Volts
P.O. Box 1111
Placentia, CA 92670
(714) 632-7721

A weekly magazine that lists only buy-and-sell ads is the *Computer Hot Line Weekly*. A subscription is $29 for 52 issues. The address is:

Computer Hot Line Weekly
Box 1373
Fort Dodge, IA 50501
1-800-247-2000

Here is a list of mail order firms who send out their catalogs free of charge:

Lyben Computer
1050 E. Maple Rd.
Troy, MI
(313) 589-3440

Priority One
21622 Plummer St.
Chatsworth, CA
(818) 709-5464

Inmac Computer Furniture
2465 St. Augustine Dr.
Santa Clara, CA 95054

Jameco Electronics
1355 Shoreway Rd.
Belmont, CA 94002
(415) 592-8097

800-SOFTWARE
940 Dwight Wy. #14
Berkeley, CA 94710
800-227-4587

Jade Computer
4901 W. Rosecrans Av.
Hawthorne, CA
(213) 973-7707

Nebs Computer Forms
500 Main St.
Groton, MA 01470
1-800-225-9550

This is not a complete listing, but it gives you an idea of what is available. Thumbing through these magazines is a great way to stay aware of what is available and do price comparisons without leaving home.

COMPUTER SHOWS

I live in San Jose, the heart of the Silicon Valley. There is a computer swap or show somewhere in the San Francisco Bay area almost every weekend. Most computer dealers, especially clone vendors, set up booths and display their wares. I enjoy the shows. There are always large crowds and a circus-like atmosphere. I often go even if I don't need anything.

There are several large shows held in San Francisco every year. One of the best is the West Coast Computer Faire, held in early spring each year. The Interface Group sponsors this show, which has exhibitors from all over the nation. The Interface Group also sponsors a Computer Faire in Boston, the Spring COMDEX (COMputer Dealers EXposition) in Atlanta, and the Fall COMDEX in Las Vegas. The Las Vegas COMDEX is the largest show in the country. It usually has about 1200 exhibitors and 80 to 100 thousand visitors.

The Las Vegas COMDEX is small compared to the international show held in Hanover, West Germany each year. In March, 1987, it had 2196 exhibitors and, despite a foot of snow on the ground, it attracted 350,000 visitors. The show was held on a fairgrounds and occupied 18 large buildings. The products were categorized and, when possible, all like products were exhibited together. IBM had exhibits in six different buildings.

Some products were exhibited there that you don't see at the computer shows in this country. Several vendors showed the latest methods of book-binding, collating, and other technologies necessary for desktop publishing. There were also exhibits of automatic addressing, labelling, and printing machines.

Many Point of Sale (POS) systems were demonstrated. These systems usually have one or more cash registers tied together with a computer.

It was impossible to see all of the exhibits in the eight days that the show was held, but it was great fun. The West Germans allow alcohol in the booths. Borland's booth had a well-stocked bar, and you could sit down, rest your feet, and have a beer or cognac while you talked business with their representatives.

I was worried while planning the trip because I do not speak German, but almost everybody that I met over there could speak some English. (If I get a chance to go next year, I hope to be able to speak a little German. I have acquired a copy of a computer program called Learn German. It is published by International Computer Products, 346 N. Western Ave., Los Angeles, CA 90004. It comes on a single floppy disk and has several German phrases that would be helpful to a traveller.)

Computers and components cost more in Europe than they do in this country. In comparison, we have some fantastic bargains here. Also, many technologies are not available in Europe until after they have been introduced here.

Considering that 350,000 people attended this show despite high prices and the cold weather, Europeans have a great interest in the computer industry.

USER GROUPS

If you live in a large city, chances are that there are several personal computer user groups (PCUGs) in your area. These groups are usually made up of people who own computers. Ordinarily, they meet once or twice a month and discuss computers, software, and problems. Some hold their meetings in a wing of the public library, in public schools, at company facilities, or at the home of one of the members.

There are several kinds of user groups. Some are set up for one particular kind of computer, such as Apple or Atari. There are several IBM PCUGs here in the Silicon Valley. I belong to a PC Clone UG. Some are set up within and sponsored by corporations. These companies realize that the more their people know about computers, the more valuable they are as employees.

A large user group can often contact local computer and software vendors and suppliers and arrange volume discounts and other benefits for the club.

If you have a problem, someone at a meeting can usually help you. Most groups publish a list of the members so you can call one of them if you have a problem. Most members are usually happy to help. I recommend you join a group. If there are none in your area, start one. There are no set rules or regulations as to how a club should be run.

Several of the magazines listed above publish lists of user groups as a public service. They also publish lists of bulletin boards (a later topic of discussion).

MODEMS

If you plan to do any serious computing, you need a modem. They are now fairly inexpensive. The two basic types are external and internal. Each type has some advantages and disadvantages.

External, desktop modems require some space and a power source. They also require a COM port and a board to drive it. Most external models have LEDs that light up and let you know what is happening during your call.

An internal modem is built entirely on a board, usually a half or short board. It plugs into one of your slots. It does not have LEDs to let you know the progress of your call, but both internal and external modems have speakers that let you hear the phone ringing or a busy signal.

The most popular modem transmission rate is the 1200 baud, but technology has advanced and costs have come down, so many people are buying 2400 baud modems. Several companies are manufacturing 9600 baud modems, and as the technology improves, that might become the next standard.

A modem plugs into your phone line. You can have a dedicated line or a Y connector as an extension off your regular line. It is not very difficult to install unless you have to crawl under the floor of your house to string an extension to your computer.

A modem is essential and worth the money, even if you have to pay someone to crawl under the floor for you.

BULLETIN BOARDS

If you have a modem, you have access to several thousand computer bulletin boards. There are over 100 here in the San Francisco Bay area. Most of them are free, but some charge a nominal fee and some ask for a tax-deductible donation.

Some bulletin boards are set up by private individuals and some by companies or vendors as a service to their customers. Some are set up by user groups and other special-interest organizations. For example, there is a gay bulletin board in the San Francisco area, an X-rated board, and several for dating.

Most bulletin boards are set up to help individuals. They usually have lots of public domain software and a space where you can leave pleas for help, advertisements, or just plain old chit-chat.

If you are just getting started, you probably need some software. Some public domain software packages are equivalent to the major commercial programs. The best part is that they are free.

Some of the programs are *shareware* such as PC-Write and QModem. You can download them and use them, but the originator asks that you send a nominal fee for the program. This is not unreasonable, considering that many of these programs are as good or better than some commercial programs that cost hundreds of dollars. They cannot force you to pay for these programs, but if you don't your conscience will probably bother you.

The bulletin boards are a two-way system. They ask you to contribute public domain software that *you* might have written or acquired so that it can be shared by other users. Most people are glad to share what they have with others.

However, there are all kinds of people in this world. Some are no-good, sadistic bastards. Some sick individuals have placed destructive "Trojan" software on bulletin boards. This software appears to be something functional and useful. It might perform for some time; then a hidden command in the software erases an entire hard disk, or it can gradually erase portions of the disk each time the machine is turned on.

Some bulletin boards have also been used for illegal and criminal activities. Stolen credit card numbers and telephone charge numbers have been left on the bulletin boards.

Because of these low-life vermin, many bulletin board system operators are now carefully checking any software that is uploaded onto their systems. Many are now restricting access to their boards, and some have started charging a fee because of the extra time it takes to monitor the boards.

There are several large national bulletin boards and information services, such as Compuserve and Dialog. My local cable TV service offers a link to my computer that provides news, stock quotations, airline schedules, and other services for a small monthly fee. Many of the national bulletin boards offer electronic mail. These services can be of great value to some individuals and businesses.

Some banks offer systems that will let you do all your banking from the comforts of your home with your computer and a modem. You would never again have to drive downtown, hunt for a parking space, and stand in line.

If you don't own a modem or the local bulletin board doesn't have the software that you need, there are several companies that will ship public domain software on a floppy disk. These companies have thousands of programs and usually charge from $3 to $24 for a disk full of programs. One company, PC-Sig has their entire library of over 20,000 files on a CD-ROM disk. They also provide CD-ROM players that will interface with a PC so that the programs can be downloaded onto a floppy or hard disk. They also provide periodic updates for the CD-ROMs.

Here is a short list of companies that provide public domain and low-cost software:

PC-Sig
1030D East Duane Ave.
Sunnyvale, CA 94086
1-800-245-6717

Software Express/Direct
Box 2288
Merrifield, VA 22116
1-800-331-8192

MicroCom Systems
P.O. Box 51657
Palo Alto, CA 94303
(415) 325-6500

Selective Software
903 Pacific Ave. Suite 301
Santa Cruz, CA 95060
1-800-423-3556

The Computer Room
P.O. Box 1596
Gordonsville, VA 22942
(703) 832-3341

National PD Library
1533 Avohill
Vista, CA 92083
(619) 941-0925

Most of the companies listed above can provide a catalog listing of their software. Some charge a small fee for their catalog. Write or call them for details and latest prices.

The above list is not complete. You might find several other companies advertised in some of the magazines listed earlier.

MAIL-ORDER COMPUTER BOOKS

One of the better ways to learn about computers is through books, but you might not be able to find the particular book you need. Several companies provide books through the mail.

TAB Books, Inc. published the book you have in your hands. TAB is one of the leading publishers of books about computers. They publish books that cover almost every aspect of computers. They also publish books that are very helpful in learning and using most of the major software programs. For a listing of their computer books, write to them at:

TAB Books, Inc
Blue Ridge Summit, PA 17294
(717) 794-2191

Another good source of computer books by mail order is InfoSource International. This company carries a large number of computer and technical book titles from several publishers. They can supply you with almost any computer or technical book that you need. Write or call for a catalog. Their address is:

InfoSource International
Box 238
Barryville, NY 12719
(717) 559-7665

15

Troubleshooting

Computers are very simple to assemble, but they have some very complex circuits and components. These circuits require very precise timing, voltages, and frequencies. Most computers operate very well for long periods of time, but nearly all of them will eventually require some sort of service.

A computer can develop a great number of problems. Some of them are easy to diagnose and repair, but some problems can be very difficult. A good technician might spend hours troubleshooting using very sophisticated equipment and still not be able to find the problem and repair the computer.

For troubleshooting computer problems, a technician usually needs a good high-frequency oscilloscope, a logic analyzer, and a good voltmeter, and the technician must be trained to use all this equipment. The technician must also have a good working knowledge of electronics and the function and purpose of each component in the computer.

Paramount Electronics of Sunnyvale has developed an automatic test instrument that can diagnose a sick PC or XT in minutes. Bill Boutin, president of Paramount Electronics, explained how this machine came to be developed. ''We import large numbers of computer components. Many of the boards and components have a very high failure rate. My bench technicians spent hours testing and troubleshooting boards before we built up our systems. Even then we would miss some of the problems and have angry customers bringing their computers back to us for repair. We discussed the problems with some of our engineers and decided that there must be an easier way. So we set about designing an instrument that would automatically check the components and circuits on a mother board. It checks all of the components and every circuit. It automatically locates and identifies any faults or failures. It even checks some plug-in boards for faults and faulty disk drives. It has saved us hundreds of hours of troubleshooting.''

They named this fantastic instrument the BLUE-ICEer. See Fig. 15-1. "ICEer" stands for In Circuit Emulator. The "BLUE" part of the name is a bit of whimsy referring to IBM, sometimes known as "Big Blue."

Besides the stand-alone version, they have also developed a board that can plug into any of the slots on a PC or XT and perform a complete circuit check-out and diagnosis.

At the present time, these instruments will only check out genuine IBM PCs, XTs, compatibles, and clones. They are working on a model that will check out an 80286 machine.

Fig. 15-1. The Paramount BLUE-ICEer, an automatic test instrument for computers.

About 10 million PCs, XTs, and clones are still in use. The BLUE-ICEer can save any computer repair or service shop hours of time and labor.

Most service and repair shops charge at least $50 an hour plus parts for computer service and repair. The cost of the parts is usually insignificant compared to the cost of the time it takes to find the problem. It can take hours to locate a defective component. The BLUE-ICEer can find them in minutes. Because the tests are all performed automatically, it takes no special training or expertise to operate the instrument. It is an instrument that every service and repair shop should have.

Before plugging in the BLUE-ICEer, make sure that the power supply of the computer under test is good. If the fan does not run when the power is turned on, two probable causes are a direct short across the mother board or a defective power supply. Most power supplies have a built-in protective circuit that shuts them down if too much current is drawn. The power supply puts out $+5$ volts, -5 volts, $+12$ volts and -12 volts. A short in any of these circuits could cause the power supply to shut down. The power connector to most mother boards is in two parts. You can unplug one part of the connector, turn the power on, and if the fan now runs, you can surmise there is a short on the mother board involving that particular voltage. If the fan doesn't run after un-plugging one-half of the connector, un-plug the other half and turn the power on again. If the fan doesn't run with both plugs disconnected, then it is probably a defective power supply. It is easy to check for the proper voltages with a simple voltmeter.

If these preliminary tests indicate there is a short on the mother board, it should be investigated further. You should look for paper clips, staples, or any other object that might have fallen into one of the board connector slots. The back side of the board should also be checked for shorts. It might be necessary to disconnect some of the large by-pass capacitors on the voltage lines and check them for shorts.

If there are no shorts, the BLUE-ICEer is then plugged into the 8088 socket and turned on. It will immediately begin testing the circuits. A computer monitor attached to the instrument shows what tests are being performed and the results.

Since most of the chips in a computer circuit work in conjunction with one another, the failure of one may cause another one to appear defective. However, at the end of the test, results of all tests are shown on the screen, and can be printed out. The chip that fails the most tests is usually defective. If this chip is replaced, and another quick test is run, the computer will usually pass all tests; the problem is fixed. On some occasions, two or three chips have to be replaced before the problem is solved. Most chips on the mother board are mounted in sockets and can be easily changed.

Computer dealers could benefit from the use of this instrument. If the computer is checked by this instrument as it is assembled, then the dealer can be more confident the customer will not be bringing it back for service.

It is very important for large corporations to keep their computers up and running. Many companies have large maintenance departments or hire service companies just for their computer upkeep. These companies can benefit from the BLUE-ICEer because it can drastically reduce the amount of down-time that the computer spends in the shop. At the present time it is available only from:

Paramount Electronics
1155 Tasman Dr.
Sunnyvale, CA 94089
(408) 734-2135

CHECKING OUT THE 80286

The BLUE-ICEer is used on the PCs and XTs. A similar diagnostic instrument should be available for the AT shortly.

The operation and interaction of the various circuits in the PC and XT is not qualitatively different than in the AT. The AT is more complex however than the PC or XT, so it is often more difficult to pinpoint a problem in the AT.

DIAGNOSTIC DISK

You should have been given a diagnostic disk by your vendor when you bought your 80286 system or mother board. If you did not, ask them for one. There is probably only a nominal fee for the disk and it is essential for setting up your computer. Without it, you can't even reset the time and date; remember, you have to do that at least twice a year, when switching to daylight saving time and back.

I have had to reset the time on my computer several times. The system time and part of the BIOS system are stored in low-power CMOS ROM chips. A battery pack supplies power to this circuit, but an anomalous condition can cause the circuit to temporarily lose power. When this happens, insert the diagnostic disk in the A: drive and boot up with it. A menu will present several options; choose number 4, Setup.

Another menu will come up and ask several questions. They are fairly straightforward. One question asks what type of hard disk you have.

You must give it the right answer, because it can be any one of 20 different types. Ask your vendor what type you have and write it down on the diagnostic disk sleeve.

Several different types of batteries are used on ATs. The IBM AT uses a battery pack that is good for about two years. It costs $30 to replace. Most clones use a pack that has four alkaline AA penlight batteries that cost about $2. They should last about three years. Some of the clones use an on-board round lithium battery. Others use a small cylindrical rechargeable battery.

There isn't too much warning when the batteries start to go dead, but if your system is over two years old and you have to frequently reset the time and date, you should change your batteries. Before you unplug the battery pack, write down the position of each colored wire and plug them back in the same way. Also, pay particular attention to the polarity of the batteries. A + marking will be on the positive side.

SUPPLY VOLTAGES

Most of the components in your computer require fairly low power and voltage. The only high voltage in your system is within the power supply and is well-enclosed. You don't have to worry about getting a shock when you open up your computer, but do worry about shocking your sensitive components with electrostatic discharge (ESD).

Before you touch the components, ground yourself and discharge any static voltage by touching the case of the computer. A person can build up an electrostatic potential of 4000 volts. If you walk across a carpet and then touch a brass doorknob, you will sometimes see a spark fly and often get a shock. On most electronic assembly lines, the workers wear a ground strap when they are working with electrostatic discharge sensitive components.

When I am installing memory chips or handling other ICs, I often use a clip lead to ground myself. I clip one end to my metal watch band and the other end to the computer case.

CHECKING SUPPLY VOLTAGES

Most power supplies have short-circuit protection. If too much load is placed on them, they will drop out and shut down like an overloaded fuse.

There are only four voltages to check for in your system. You can do it with a volt-ohmmeter. There should be +5 volts, −5 volts, +12 volts and −12 volts. These voltages should be found on the 12-pin connector to the mother board, on the connector pins for disk drive power, and on the same pin number on each of the eight slots. Tables 15-1 and 15-2 show where the pin voltages should be found.

Pin	Color	Function
1	Yellow	+ 12 Vdc
2	Black	Ground
3	Black	Ground
4	Red	+ 5 Vdc

Table 15-1. Disk Drive Power Supply Connections.

The eight slotted connectors on the mother board each have 62 contacts, 31 on the A side and 31 on the B side. The black ground wires connect to B1 of each of the eight slots. B3 and B29 has + 5 Vdc; B5, − 5 Vdc; B7, − 12 Vdc; and B9, + 12 Vdc.

COOLING

The fan in the power supply should provide all the cooling that is needed. If you have stuffed your computer into a corner and piled things around it, shutting off all its circulation, it could overheat. Heat is an enemy of semiconductors, so try to give them plenty of breathing room.

I mentioned earlier that the fan pulls air through the front grill and sweeps it over the components, into the power supply box, and out the back of the power supply. All other openings into the computer should be covered. All unused slots should have blanks installed on the back panel so that the air will be forced out through the power supply.

REPAIR AND MAINTENANCE

Once a system is up and running, you should have no more trouble from it than you would expect from a genuine IBM. Most vendors give at least a 90-day warranty. If a disk drive or a board becomes defective

Table 15-2. Power Supply Connections to Mother Board.

	Pin	Color	Function
P8	1	White	Power Good
	2	No connection	
	3	Yellow	+ 12 Vdc
	4	Brown	− 12 Vdc
	5	Black	Ground
	6	Black	Ground
P9	1	Black	Ground
	2	Black	Ground
	3	Blue	− 5 Vdc
	4	Red	+ 5 Vdc
	5	Red	+ 5 Vdc
	6	Red	+ 5 Vdc

after this time, it might be best to pull it out, throw it away, and install a new one. Most computer repair shops charge at least $50 an hour for service. It might be a good idea to have a spare disk drive and a couple boards on hand. If something goes wrong, you can plug in a new board and see if the problem goes away. Some people might be afraid to change a board, but it is really very simple.

If you have a hard disk, don't jar it, especially while it is running. This could cause a head crash.

INSTRUMENTS AND TOOLS

There are different levels of troubleshooting. You would need sophisticated and expensive instruments to do a thorough analysis of a system. A good high frequency oscilloscope, a digital analyzer, and a logic probe are necessary. You would also need a test bench with a power supply, disk drives, and a computer with some empty slots so that you could plug in suspect boards and test them.

Other necessary tools include a volt-ohmmeter, some clip leads, a pair of diagonal cutters, a pair of needle nose pliers, screwdrivers, nutdrivers, a soldering iron and solder, and many different-sized screws and nuts. You will need plenty of light over the bench and a small flashlight to light up the dark places in the case. Most important, you need a lot of training and experience.

COMMON PROBLEMS

For most of the common problems, you won't need all that gear. I have found that a large percentage of my problems is due to my own errors. Many are caused by not taking the time to read the instructions (or not being able to understand them).

Often a problem can be solved by using your eyes, ears, nose and touch. If you look closely, you might find a cable is not plugged in properly, a board is not completely seated, or a switch is not set right. You can use your ears to detect any unusual sounds. The only sound from your computer should be the noise of your disk drive motors and the fan in the power supply. You will never forget the smell of a burned resistor or capacitor. If you smell something very unusual, try to locate where it is coming from. If you touch the components and some seem to be unusually hot, it could be the cause of your problem. Be cautious around the power supply for the incoming 110-volt line voltage.

RECOMMENDED TOOLS

You should have some tools around the house, even if you never have any computer problems. This includes several sizes of screwdrivers. A couple of them should be magnetic for picking up and starting small screws. You can buy magnetic screwdrivers or you can make one yourself. Take a strong magnet and rub it on the blade of the screwdriver a few times. Remember to be careful with magnets around your floppy disk—it can erase them.

You should also have a small screwdriver with a bent tip, which can be used to pry up ICs. Some larger ICs are very difficult to remove. A large spring paper clip is ideal for installing chips, especially the small memory type.

You should have a couple pairs of pliers, including at least one pair of long nose pliers. You will need a pair of diagonal cutters for clipping component leads wire. You can buy cutters that also have wire strippers.

A soldering iron and solder always come in handy. Also, no home should be without a volt-ohmmeter. They can be used to check the wiring in house wall sockets. (The wide slot should be ground.) Use to check wiring continuity in your car, house, stereo, and phone lines, and you can also check for the proper voltages in your computer. You can buy a relatively inexpensive volt-ohmmeter at any Radio Shack or other electronics stores.

You should also have several clip leads, also available at Radio Shack. Finally, get a good flashlight to look into dark places inside the computer.

HOW TO FIND THE PROBLEM

Always make a diagram of the wires, cables and switch settings before you disturb them. It is easy to forget how they were plugged in or set before you moved them and you could end up making things worse.

CAUTION! Always turn off the power when plugging in or unplugging a board or cable.

If it seems to be a problem on the mother board or a plug-in board, look for chips that have the same number. Try swapping them to see if the problem goes away or worsens. if you suspect a board and you have a spare or can borrow one, swap it.

If you suspect a board but don't know which one, take the boards out to the barest minimum. Then replace them one at a time until the problem surfaces.

Wiggle the boards and cables to see if it is an intermittent problem. Many times, a wire can be broken and still maintain contact until it is moved. Check the ICs and connectors for bent pins. If you have just installed memory ICs and get errors, check to make sure they are seated properly.

You can also try unplugging a cable or board and plugging it back in. If the problem is in a DIP switch, you might try turning it on and off a few times.

If you are having monitor problems, check the switch settings on the mother board. The XT has a DIP switch that must be set for monochrome or color, and the AT has a small slide switch. Most monitors also have fuses, so check them. Also check the cables for proper connections.

Printer problems, especially serial printer problems, are so numerous that I will not even attempt to list them here. Many printers today offer both parallel and serial operation. IBM defaults to the parallel system. If possible, use the parallel port. Parallel interfaces have very few problems.

Most printers have a self test. Your printer might run this test fine, but then have no response to the computer. Check the cables, parity, and baud rate.

Sometimes, the computer will hang up. You might have told it to do something that it could not do. You can usually do a warm reboot by pressing CTRL, ALT, and DEL. This wipes out any file in RAM. Occasionally, the computer will not respond to a warm boot. In that case, switch off the main power, let it sit for a few seconds, and then power up again.

DOS has several error messages, but many of them are vague. The DOS manual explains some of them, but you might want to get a book that goes into more detail.

If you find the problem is a board, a disk drive, or some other hardware, you should find out what it would cost before having it repaired. With the low-cost clone hardware that is available, it is often less expensive to scrap a defective part and buy a new one.

Glossary

access time—The amount of time it takes the computer to find and read data from a disk or from memory.

adapter boards or cards—The plug-in boards needed to drive monitors.

algorithm—A step-by-step procedure, scheme, formula or method used to solve a problem or accomplish a task. Can be a subroutine in a software program.

alphanumeric—Data that has both numerals and letters.

ANSI—American National Standard Institute. A standard adopted by MS-DOS for cursor positioning. It is used in the ANSI.SYS file for device drivers.

ASCII—American Standard Code for Information Interchange. Binary numbers from 0 to 127 that represent the upper and lowercase letters of the alphabet, the numerals 0-9, and several symbols found on a keyboard. A block of eight 0's and 1's (*bits*) are used to represent all of these characters (a *byte*). The first 32 characters, 0 through 31, are reserved for non-character functions of a keyboard, modem, printer, or other device. Number 32, or 0010 0000, represents the space, which is a character. The numeral one is represented by the binary number for 49, which is 0011 0001. Text written in ASCII is displayed on the computer screen as standard text. Text written in other systems, such as WordStar, has several other characters added and is more difficult to read. Another 128 character representations have been added to the original 128 for graphics and programming purposes.

ASIC—An acronym for Application Specific Integrated Circuit.

asynchronous—A serial type of communication where one bit at a time is transmitted. The bits are usually sent in blocks of eight 0's and 1's (a *byte*).

autoexec.bat—If present, this file is run automatically by DOS after it boots up. It is a file that can load and run certain programs or configure your system.

BASIC—Beginners All-Purpose Symbolic Instruction Code. A high-level language that was once very popular. There are still many programs and games that use it.

.BAK files—When you edit or change a file in some word processors and other software programs, they save the original file as a backup and append the extension {.BAK} to it.

batch—The batch command can be used to link commands and run them automatically. The batch commands can easily be made up by the user. They all have the extension {.bat}.

baud—A measurement of the speed or data transfer rate of a communications line. Most present-day modems operate at 1200 baud. This equals 1200 its per second or about 120 characters per second.

benchmark—A standard type program against which similar programs can be compared.

bi-directional—Both directions. Most printers print in both directions, saving the time it takes to return to the other end of a line.

binary—Numbers that use two as their base and are represented by 1's and 0's.

BIOS—An acronym for Basic Input/Output System.

bits—A contraction of Binary and digITs. These 1's and 0's represent all data that is manipulated by a computer and other digital devices.

boot or bootstrap—When a computer is turned on, the memory and internal operators have to be set or configured. The IBM takes quite a while to boot up because it checks all the memory parity and most of the peripherals. A small amount of the program to do this is stored in ROM. The computer "pulls itself up by its bootstraps." A "warm" boot is sometimes necessary if the computer is hung up for some reason. A warm boot can be done by pressing CTRL, ALT and DEL.

bubble memory—A non-volatile memory that is created by the magnetization of small bits of ferrous material. It held promise at one time, but is expensive to make and is slower than semiconductor memory.

buffer—A buffer is usually some discrete amount of memory that is used to hold data temporarily. A computer can send data thousands of times faster than a printer or modem can utilize it, but in many cases the computer can do nothing until all data has been transferred. The data can be loaded into a buffer, which then feeds the data into the printer as needed. The computer is then free to do other tasks.

bug, debug—The early computers were made with high-voltage vacuum tubes. It took rooms full of hot tubes to do the job that a credit card calculator can do today. One day, one of the larger systems went down. After several hours of troubleshooting, the technicians found a large bug that had crawled into the high-voltage wiring. It had been electrocuted and was shorting out the whole system. Since that time, any type of trouble in a piece of software or hardware is called a bug. To debug is to find errors or defects and correct them.

bulletin boards—Usually a computer with a hard disk that can be accessed with a modem. Software and programs can be uploaded or left on the bulletin board by a caller, or a caller can scan the software that has been left there by others and download any that he likes. The BB's often have help and message services. A great source of help for a beginner.

bus—Wires or circuits that connect a number of devices together. It can also be a system. The IBM PC bus is the configuration of the circuits that connect the 62 pins of the 8 slots together on the mother board. It has become the de facto standard for the clones and compatibles.

byte—A byte is eight bits, or a block of eight 0's and 1's. These eight bits can be arranged in 256 (2^8) different ways. Therefore, one byte can be made to represent any one of the 256 characters in the ASCII character set (it takes one byte to make a single character).

cache memory—A high-speed buffer set up to hold data that is being read or written to disks.

cell—A place for a single unit of data in memory, or an address in a spreadsheet.

Centronics parallel port—A system of eight-bit parallel transmission first used by the Centronics Company. It has become a standard and is the default method of printer output on the IBM.

character—A letter, a number, or a byte of data.

chip—An integrated circuit, usually made from a silicon wafer. It is microscopically etched and can have thousands of transistors and semiconductors in a very small area. The 80286 CPU used in the AT has 120,000 transistors in it.

clock—The operations of a computer are based on very precise timing, so they use a crystal to control their internal clocks. The standard frequency for the PC and XT is 4.77 million cycles per second (Hertz). The turbo systems operate at 6 to 8 MHz.

cluster—Two or more sectors on a track of a disk.

composite video—A less expensive monitor that combines all the colors in a single input line.

console—In the early days, a monitor and keyboard was usually set up at a desk-like console. The term stuck. A console is a computer. The command {COPY CON} allows you to use the keyboard as a typewriter. Type {COPY CON PRN} or {COPY CON LPT1} and everything you type will be sent to the printer. At the end of your file, type {Ctrl Z} or {F6} to stop sending.

co-processor—Usually an 8087 or 80287 that works in conjunction with the CPU and vastly speeds up some operations.

copy protection—A system that prevents a disk from being copied.

CPU—Central processing unit, such as the 8088 or 80286.

current directory—The directory that is in use at the time.

cursor—The blinking spot on the screen that indicates where next character will appear.

daisy wheel—A round printer or typewriter wheel with flexible fingers that has the alphabet and other formed characters.

data base—A collection of data, usually related in some way.

DATE **command**—The date will be displayed anytime {DATE} is typed at the the prompt sign.

DMA—Direct Memory Access. Some parts of the computer, such as the disk drives, can exchange data directly with the RAM without having to go through the CPU.

documentation—Manuals, instructions or specifications for a system, hardware, or software.

dumb terminal—A terminal that does not have its own microprocessor.

ECHO—A command that causes information to be displayed on the screen.

EEMS—Enhanced Expanded Memory Specification. A specification for adding expanded memory put forth by AST, Quadram and Ashton-Tate. (AQA EEMS).

EEPROM—An Electrically Erasable Programmable Read Only Memory chip.

EGA—Enhanced Graphics Adapter. Board used for high-resolution monitors.

EMS—Expanded Memory Specification. A specification for adding expanded memory put forth by Lotus, Intel, and Microsoft (LIM EMS).

EPROM—An Erasable Programmable Read Only Memory chip.

ergonomics—The study of how the human body can be the most productive in working with machinery.

errors—DOS displays several error messages if it receives bad commands or there are problems of some sort.

expanded memory—Memory that can be added to a PC, XT, or AT. It can only be accessed through special software.

expansion boards—Boards that can be plugged into one of the slots on the mother board to add memory or other functions.

extended memory—Memory that can be added to an 80286 or 80386 that will be addressable with the OS/2 operating system.

external commands—DOS commands that are not loaded into memory when the computer is booted.

FAT—An acronym for the File Application Table. This is a table that DOS uses to keep track of all of the parts of a file.

fonts—The different types of print letters, such as Gothic, Courier, Roman, or Italic.

fragmentation—If a disk has several records that have been changed several times, there are bits of the files on several different tracks and sectors. This slows down writing and reading of the files because the head has to move back and forth to the various tracks. If these files are copied to a newly formatted disk, each file will be written to clean tracks that are contiguous. This will decrease the access time to the disk.

friction feed—A printer that uses a roller or platen to pull the paper through.

game port—An input/output (I/O) port for joysticks, trackballs, paddles and other devices.

gigabyte—One billion bytes. This will soon be a common memory size. In virtual mode, the 80286 can address this much memory.

glitch—An unexpected electrical spike or static disturbance that can cause loss of data.

global—Something that appears throughout an entire document or program.

handshaking—A protocol or routine between systems, usually the printer and the computer, to indicate readiness to communicate with each other.

hexadecimal—A system that uses base 16. Our binary system is based on 2, our decimal is based on 10.

hidden files—The files that do not show up in a normal directory display.

high-level language—A language such as BASIC, Pascal, or C. These program languages are fairly easy to read and understand.

ICs—integrated circuits. The first integrated circuit was two transistors in a single can early in the 1960s.

interface—A piece of hardware or a set of rules that allows communications between two systems.

internal commands—Those commands that are loaded into memory when DOS boots up.

interpreter—A program that translates a high-level language into machine readable code.

kilobyte—1000 bytes, or more exactly, 1024 bytes. This is 2 to the 10th power.

LAN—An acronym for local area network. Several computers are tied together or to a central server.

low-level language—A machine-level language. Usually in binary digits. Difficult to read as compared to high-level language.

LQ—Letter-quality print, found with daisy wheel or formed type printers.

mainframe—A large computer that can serve several users.

megabyte—1,000,000 bytes, or 1 M. More precisely, 2 to the 20th power, (2^9) or 1,048,576 bytes.

menu—A list of choices or options. A menu-driven system makes it very easy for beginners to choose what they want to run or do.

MFM—Modified Frequency Modulation. The standard method of recording on hard disks. See RLL.

MODE—A DOS command that must be invoked to direct the computer output to a serial printer.

mouse—A small pointing device that can control the cursor. It usually has two or three buttons that are assigned various functions.

NLQ—An acronym for near letter quality. The modified, improved characters of a dot-matrix printer.

null modem cable—A cable with certain pairs of wires crossed over. If the computer sends data from pin 2, the modem may receive it on pin 3. The modem would send data back to the computer from its pin 2 and be received by the computer on pin 3. Several other wires would also be crossed.

OS/2—The long-awaited operating system that should allow 80286 and 80386 machines to directly address huge amounts of memory. It should remove many of the limitations that DOS now imposes.

parallel—A system that uses eight lines to send eight bits at a time.
plotter—An X-Y writing device that can be used for charts, graphics, and many other functions that most printers can't do.
prompt—The sign that shows that DOS is waiting for an entry.

RAM—Random access memory. Volatile memory.
RGB—For red, green and blue, the three primary colors that are used in color monitors and TVs. Each color has its own electron gun that shoots a stream of electrons to the back of the monitor screen and causes it to light up in various colors.
RLL—Run length limited. A scheme of hard disk recording that allows 50 percent more data to be recorded on a hard disk than the standard MFM scheme allows. ERLL, or Enhanced RLL allows twice as much data to be recorded on a hard disk.
ROM—Read only memory, which is non-volatile.

sector—A section of a track on a disk.
serial—The transmission of one bit at a time over a single line.
source—The origin or disk to be copied from.
SPOOL—Simultaneous Peripheral Operations On-Line. A software-invoked RAM partition that functions as a large buffer.

target—The disk to be copied to.
time stamp—The record of the time and date that is stored in the directory when a file is created or changed.
tractor—A printer device with sprockets or spikes that pulls computer paper by the holes in the margins through the printer at a very precise feed rate. Opposingly, a friction-feed platen can allow the paper to slip or move to one side or the other, allowing possible fluctuation of spacing.
turbo—Usually means a computer with faster-than-normal speed.

virtual—Something that might be apparently, but not physically, present. If you have a single disk drive, it will be drive {A:}, but you also hae a virtual drive {B} if your DIP switches on the mother board are set properly.
volatile—Refers to memory units that lose stored information when power is off.

Windows—Many new software packages are now loaded into memory. They stay in the background until they are called for, and then they pop up on the screen in a window. Also, the Microsoft company has a software package called Windows. It provides an operating environment for many DOS programs.

Index

Edited by Lisa A. Doyle

Other Bestsellers Form TAB